To Jill

Food like life is a journey to enjoy

Annette Fear

THE BEST OF
Spirit House

THE BEST OF
Spirit House

Helen Brierty and Annette Fear

NH
NEW
HOLLAND

Contents

Introduction

Do you have a favourite food memory? Your first oyster, or glass of champagne, harvesting a first crop of home grown carrots or tomatoes, your first meal in a five star 'hatted' restaurant, or barbecuing freshly caught fish on the beach under a summer moon?

For us, our most memorable meal, still discussed with nostalgic pleasure, was a simple oyster omelette in Singapore in the late 1970s. It was our first trip to Asia. Arriving after dark, jet lagged, exhausted, we checked into a hotel then went for a walk in a nearby park to ease stiffened legs. Here we stumbled upon a food vendor cooking smoky oyster omelettes on a hot plate over glowing charcoal. Sitting on the side of the pavement, eating off a paper plate, overwhelmed by the humidity of the night and wafts of tropical vegetation, Peter remarked that he had never felt more at home. A definite case of love at first bite. Welcome to Asia.

Over the next 40 years, we travelled extensively through Malaysia, China, Indonesia, Bali, Vietnam, Cambodia, but most especially in Thailand, which became our home away from home. From that simple oyster omelette, we gradually delved into the regional flavours and exotic ingredients of many Asian cuisines. The more we travelled, the more we came to understand the impact of Arabic, Chinese, Portuguese, Indian, Japanese, Dutch and French traders on the local food.

Spirit House Restaurant and Cooking School, is the outcome of this personal journey in Asian food—even though it took many years to eventuate. Opening in 1995, originally planned as a semi retirement hobby (stop laughing) Spirit House has grown into an iconic destination for lovers of Asian food. The five acres of tropical gardens are surrounded by farmers growing ginger, galangal, turmeric, papaya, kaffir limes, lemongrass, chillies, Thai basil and coriander (cilantro). Add into this mix freshly caught prawns (shrimp), tuna, reef fish, scallops, squid and crabs from local trawlers, organic poultry or pork—and you can appreciate why our chefs consider themselves culinary blessed.

This book is the culmination of twenty years working together with our first Head Chef, Annette Fear. Having travelled and studied food for years across South East Asia, word gradually spread about the fragrant, Thai inspired menus Annette was creating at Spirit House. With an encyclopedic knowledge of Asian ingredients and their history, plus being an avid home gardener of exotic herbs and vegetables, Annette set a very high bar for the many chefs who have followed in her footsteps over ensuing years.

Annette was the inspiration behind the Spirit House Cooking School as she is a natural teacher, with a gift for creating recipes for home cooks which demystify Asian ingredients and cooking methods. Teaching classes every week has given Annette a unique insight into what Australian families like to eat and how they choose to entertain. The following recipes certainly illustrate her knowledge and skills and hopefully will inspire you to recreate them for the enjoyment of your family and friends.

Spirit House is more than just a family business—it is a tight knit community of over fifty, talented staff who take pride in ensuring its continued success. Without their contribution and enthusiasm, our restaurant dream would have remained just that. Heartfelt thanks to each and every one of you for travelling with us on this remarkable Spirit House journey.

Helen & Peter Brierty

Starters

Miang of Spanner Crab, Coconut, Mint & Pomelo

Miang in Thai means 'to wrap' and miang can use lettuce, wild pepper leaves, thin omelette or freshly steamed rice noodles, to name just a few 'wraps'. My first experience of miang was at the Bangkok weekend market, where I came across an old woman who had a selection of ingredients in a large enamel bowl. She made me a very common snack called Miang Cha Plu which refers to the wild pepper leaf used in this variation. After smearing the leaf with a sweet sauce, she added a piece or two of ginger, lime, peanut, chilli, roasted coconut, lemongrass and dried prawns (shrimp). It was all eaten in one bite, giving me my first experience of the Thai rainbow effect, where all the flavours explode at once and you get the amazing interplay of the different ingredients. And to think something this good was just a simple snack!

The cha plu leaf comes from the pepper family and is often referred to as wild betel leaf, being from the same family as the betel leaf used for chewing. These plants are found growing wild and in gardens throughout Asia. The leaves should be available in Asian grocery stores. If unavailable, use baby spinach leaves or soft lettuce.

This recipe is a very glamourised version of the everyday miang, but still uses many of the traditional elements. If the thought of picking over crabmeat is too much (and it must be fresh crab), then use cooked prawns (shrimp).

INGREDIENTS:

16 wild pepper leaves

200g (7 oz) fresh crabmeat, picked over to remove traces of shell

2 tablespoons young ginger, peeled and finely shredded

2 tablespoons shredded fresh coconut

¼ cup mint leaves

1 cup pomelo or grapefruit chunks, with all skin and pith removed

2 stalks lemongrass, finely sliced, bottom half only and tough outer leaves removed

4 kaffir lime leaves, shredded into fine slivers

½ red chilli, de-seeded (pitted) and finely shredded

¼ cup coriander (cilantro) leaves

DRESSING

1 teaspoon roasted chilli paste

1 teaspoon light palm sugar

1 tablespoon fish sauce

3 tablespoons lime juice

2 tablespoons coconut cream

Serves 8

METHOD:

In a bowl, combine the crabmeat, ginger, coconut, mint, pomelo, lemongrass and kaffir lime leaves. Add the dressing and toss gently to combine. Divide the crab between the pepper leaves and garnish with chilli strips and coriander leaves.

TO MAKE DRESSING:

Combine all ingredients in a bowl and stir to combine.

Shitake Mushroom Wontons with Shallot Oil

A popular steamed vegetarian entrée from the Spirit House restaurant menu.

INGREDIENTS:

400 g (14 oz) dried shitake mushrooms (soaked in warm water & drained)

10 ml (½ fl oz) vegetable oil

25 g (¾ oz) pounded garlic

30 g (1 oz) carrot, finely chopped

50 g (1½ oz) bamboo shoots, finely chopped

50 g (1½ oz) bean spouts, finely chopped

50 g (1½ oz) snow peas (mange tout), finely chopped

1 teaspoon ground white pepper

1 tablespoon chopped coriander (cilantro) root

50 g (1½ oz) light palm sugar, crushed

60 ml (2 fl oz) light soy sauce

50 wonton skins, defrosted

1 egg beaten

75 g (2½ oz) unsalted cashew nuts, cooked and chopped

2 tablespoons shallot oil

2 tablespoons soy sauce

2 tablespoons sesame seeds

Serves 6–8

METHOD:

Chop mushrooms in a food processor until finely minced.

Heat vegetable oil in a wok. Cook garlic gently on low heat. Add chopped vegetables and cook until soft.

Mix in chopped mushrooms, white pepper, coriander root, palm sugar and soy sauce and cook over a moderate heat for 5 minutes. Place on tray to cool and fold through chopped cashew nuts.

TO MAKE WONTONS:

Place wonton skins on a bench a few at a time. Brush lightly with beaten egg and place a second skin overlapping diagonally. Place wonton skin in a dariole mould and place 1½ tablespoons of mushroom mix into each of the moulds. Press mixture until firm using another mould. Don't close the wontons at the top, but leave open.

Turn out and place into bamboo steamer to cook.

Steam wontons over rapidly boiling water for 6–7 minutes.

Serve with shallot oil, soy sauce and toasted sesame seeds.

TO MAKE SHALLOT OIL:

2 golden shallots, peeled and sliced

1 cup flavourless vegetable oil e.g. peanut

Heat oil to moderately hot and fry the shallots until golden, remove from oil.

The shallots are used as a crunchy garnish and the oil is used as a flavouring to finsh many dishes.

Seared Scallops, Pickled Vegetables with Chilli, Soybean & Tamarind Sauce

A stunning entrée that perfectly demonstrates the Thai balance of flavours.

PICKLED VEGETABLES:

1 medium carrot

½ red capsicum (sweet pepper)

½ gold capsicum (sweet pepper)

12 baby corn

1 small red onion

1 cucumber

2 green chilli, sliced

25 g (¾ oz) finely sliced ginger

200 ml (7 fl oz) rice wine vinegar

250 g (8 oz) palm sugar

1 tablespoon fish sauce

SAUCE:

250 g (8 oz) chilli paste & soy bean oil (available in jar from Asian supermarkets)

60 ml (2 fl oz) tamarind water

50 ml (1¾ fl oz) tomato ketchup

150 ml (5 fl oz) coconut cream

1 tablespoon sugar

12 Tasmanian scallops in half shell (roe off)

10 ml (½ fl oz) vegetable oil

finely sliced chilli and coriander (cilantro) to garnish

rock salt & Szechwan peppercorns to garnish

Serves 4

TO MAKE PICKLED VEGETABLES:

Cut carrots, capsicums, baby corn and red onion into strips approximately the same size. Place into a bowl with the green chilli and ginger.

Bring rice wine vinegar, fish sauce and palm sugar to a simmer until the sugar has dissolved. Cool slightly and pour over vegetables. Allow vegetables to pickle for a few hours.

TO MAKE SAUCE:

In a heavy based pot, sauté chilli paste until fragrant. Add tamarind water, sugar and tomato ketchup and simmer for 5 minutes. Add coconut cream and simmer for a further 5 minutes.

Remove scallops from half shells. Pan fry scallops in vegetable oil until caramelised but still slightly undercooked. Place a few spoons of the prepared chilli and tamarind sauce in the pan and finish cooking until scallops are firm.

TO SERVE:

Clean scallop shells and arrange on a bed of rock salt with some Szechwan pepper corns mixed through. Place a small amount of the vegetable pickle in each shell and then one scallop. Finish with reduced sauce and garnish with coriander and chilli.

Steamed Prawn & Chicken Dumplings

A popular street side snack, these dumplings are a wonderful starter for a Thai-style meal or just as a snack with drinks. They are accented with three great condiments: Sweet Black Bean Sauce, Si Racha chilli sauce (or any hot sweet chilli sauce) and Golden Fried Garlic

INGREDIENTS:

250 g (8 oz) chicken mince (ground)

250 g (8 oz) green prawn meat, finely chopped

2 green spring onions (scallions), including some of the green top, finely chopped

1 cup water chestnuts, finely chopped

4 cloves garlic, crushed with a pinch of salt in a mortar with a pestle

1 egg

2 tablespoons fish sauce

1 tablespoon oyster sauce

1 teaspoon ground white pepper

1 tablespoon light palm sugar

1 packet wonton wrappers

1 egg, beaten and mixed with a tablespoon of water

SWEET BLACK BEAN SAUCE:

½ cup (125 ml/4 fl oz) kecap manis (sweet soy sauce)

¼ cup (60 ml/2 fl oz) coconut vinegar

¼ cup (60 g/2 oz) dark palm sugar

GOLDEN FRIED GARLIC:

½ cup (125 ml/4 fl oz) vegetable oil

10 cloves garlic, sliced thinly and evenly

Makes about 35

METHOD:

Mix all ingredients together until well combined. Fill wontons with about 1 dessertspoon of mix. Brush edges of wonton with a little egg wash and close the sides.

Fill a large wok half full of water and bring to the boil. Place wontons in a bamboo steamer basket and then place the basket in the wok over boiling water. Cover and cook for about 10–15 minutes, then transfer to serving platter.

To serve, spoon a little Golden Fried Garlic with its oil over the wontons, then a drizzle of Sweet Black Bean Sauce and some Si Racha chilli sauce to taste.

TO MAKE SI RACHA SAUCE:

A sweet hot sauce that comes from the seaside port of Si Racha, but any hot sweet chilli sauce would work with these dumplings. Buy Si Racha sauce in Asian supermarkets.

TO MAKE SWEET BLACK BEAN SAUCE:

Combine all ingredients in a small pan and bring to the boil. Stir until sugar dissolves. Remove from heat. Keeps for weeks in the refrigerator. Best warmed slightly before serving.

Golden Fried Garlic

Used frequently to garnish all sorts of dishes. It does require a bit of care, because if the oil is too hot, the garlic becomes bitter and acrid. So don't overheat the oil and remove garlic when it's just starting to turn pale golden.

TO MAKE GOLDEN FRIED GARLIC:

Heat oil to moderate and fry garlic until it's aromatic and pale golden, about 2 minutes. Remove from heat, stirring as the pan cools. Refrigerate until needed. Keeps about 1 week in the refrigerator.

Crispy Prawn Wontons with Pork & Basil

These have been a favourite at the restaurant and cooking school over the years. The pork stuffing is seasoned with classic red curry paste. This dish can be simplified by omitting the stuffing and just wrapping the prawn (shrimp) in a basil leaf and then wrapping it again in the wonton pastry. Like most deep-fried foods, these are best served with a sweet-and-sour style sauce like sweet chilli.

INGREDIENTS:

125 g (4 oz) pork mince, ground

1 teaspoon red curry paste

2 kaffir lime leaves, finely shredded

1 teaspoon fish sauce

pinch white sugar

1 green spring onion (scallion), white part
   only, finely chopped

2 tablespoons coriander (cilantro) leaves
   and stems, finely chopped

16 large basil leaves for wrapping

16 large green prawns (shrimp),
   deveined, tail on and butterflied

16 square wonton wrappers

1 egg, lightly beaten and mixed with a
   tablespoon of water

2 cups (500 ml/17 fl oz) vegetable oil

Sweet Chilli Dipping Sauce (see page
   109)

Serves 8 as part of a selection of dishes

METHOD:

Combine pork mince, curry paste, lime leaf, fish sauce, sugar, green spring onion and coriander leaves. Mix well. Place the pork mince in a piping bag and pipe 1 teaspoon of the mix down the back of each prawn. (If a piping bag is not available, you can spoon 1 teaspoon of mix down the back of the prawn.) Now wrap 1 basil leaf around the stuffed prawn, and then wrap the prawn in a wonton, leaving the tail protruding. Seal with an egg wash.

Heat vegetable oil in wok to medium heat and deep-fry the prawns until the wonton pastry is golden and the prawns cooked through, about 3–5 minutes.

Transfer to a serving plate and serve with sweet chilli dipping sauce.

Steamed Sesame & Ginger Prawns

This simple and quick dish relies on the quality of the seafood. I recommend spending the extra money and buying Australian wild caught prawns (shrimp) for the best result. It would be unthinkable in Asia to serve such expensive seafood without the head. Along with the legs, the head has lots of flavour. Ironically, a lot of Westerners find the head off-putting, and wouldn't order the dish if the prawns weren't peeled and heads removed.

INGREDIENTS:

12 large king prawns (shrimp), peeled, de-veined but with tail and heads left on (optional)

2 tablespoons oyster sauce

2 tablespoons ginger, finely shredded

1 large green chilli, de-seeded (pitted) and julienned

2 green spring onions (scallions), finely sliced, including some of the green part

½ teaspoon ground white pepper

2 tablespoons soy sauce

2 tablespoons Shaoxing wine

2 tablespoons peanut oil

1 tablespoon sesame oil

¼ cup coriander (cilantro) leaves

Serves 4, or 8 as part of a selection of dishes

METHOD:

Toss prawns with oyster sauce and place in a bamboo steamer basket lined with baking paper. Place basket over a wok of rapidly boiling water and steam, covered, for about 8–10 minutes or until just cooked.

Transfer to a serving plate and cover with the ginger, chilli, spring onions and pepper. Combine the soy sauce and Shaoxing wine and sprinkle over the prawns. In a small saucepan, combine the peanut and sesame oils. Heat until almost smoking, then pour over the prawns. Garnish with the coriander leaves before serving.

Seafood Noodle Balls with Sweet Chilli Sauce

What's not to love – spicy seafood balls encased in crunchy noodles, drizzled with sweet chilli sauce.

INGREDIENTS:

200 g (7 oz) prawn (shrimp) meat,
  roughly chopped
200 g (7 oz) squid, roughly chopped
1 red onion, sliced Chinese style
½ cup chopped coriander
  (cilantro) stems
1 tablespoon garlic, finely chopped
1 tablespoon ginger, finely chopped
2 eggs, beaten
½ cup plain flour
fish sauce to season
freshly ground white pepper
1 teaspoon sambal olek
2 bundles dried egg noodles, soaked in
  warm water until soft, drained, cut into
  5 cm (2 in) pieces

Serves 4

METHOD:

Place all of the ingredients in large bowl and mix thoroughly until well combined.

Heat 2 cups vegetable oil in wok. Drop teaspoons of mixture into hot oil and cook until golden brown, about 5 minutes. Don't make the balls too large or they will be doughy in the middle. Drain on paper towel.

Serve with Sweet Chilli Sauce (see recipe page 109)

Pork Belly with Citrus Caramel Sauce

An all-time, mouth watering favourite from the restaurant menu.
If you are a keen cook, this Chinese master stock is well worth the making. Once started, master stock can be used over and over again for poaching fish, poultry and meat. The stock can be reduced down to make a rich, luscious sauce. In China, master stocks can be handed down within families as wedding presents – the stock can be generations old because it is continually boiled and added to in readiness for the next use.

MASTER STOCK:

2 L (3½ pints) of water

250 ml (8 fl oz) shaoxing wine

125 ml (4 fl oz) light soy sauce

75 ml (2½ fl oz) dark soy sauce

100 g (3½ oz) yellow rock sugar

2 pieces tangerine peel

2 pieces cassia bark

4 pieces star anise

1 knob of ginger, roughly chopped

4 cloves garlic

PORK:

2 L (3½ pints) masterstock

1 kg (2.2 lb) pork belly, bone out and skin on

1 L (34 fl oz) vegetable oil

TO MAKE MASTER STOCK:

Bring all ingredients to boil in a large stock pot, simmer for 1 hour. Strain. Portion into smaller quantities and freeze. Use as base for soups, add a few spoonfuls to a stir-fry or use for braising meats.

TO COOK PORK:

Preheat oven to 175°C (325°F/Gas Mark 3). Bring master stock to boil then pour over the belly, skin side up, in a tray. Cover the tray with foil and place in the oven for 2 hours. Remove from oven, allow pork to cool in the stock. Pour off stock and reserve for future use. Refrigerate pork belly overnight.

TO SERVE:

Cut the pork into 4 cm (1½ in) pieces. Heat oil to medium in large wok. Once oil is ready, place 4–6 pieces of pork in oil and fry until golden brown or crispy. Drain pork on paper towel and serve. Keep warm while you repeat the process with remaining pieces.

NOTE: take extreme care when deep frying the pork, as it can splatter. Cover the wok with a bamboo steamer basket lid, or a sheet of loose foil, to prevent splashing.

Recipe continues on page 29

CITRUS CARAMEL SAUCE:

4 coriander (cilantro) roots

50 g (1¾ oz) ginger

30 g (1 oz) fresh turmeric

500 ml (16 fl oz) fresh citrus juice
    (mandarin or orange)

500 g (17½ oz) palm sugar

50 ml (1¾ fl oz) water

4 kaffir lime leaves

2 star anise

1 piece cassia bark

1 lemon grass stalk

HERB GARNISH:

1 cup coriander (cilantro) leaves

1 cup mint leaves

2 tablespoons finely shredded ginger

1 stalk lemongrass, finely sliced

1 large red chill, deseeded and finely
    sliced

2 tablespoons fish sauce

2 tablespoons lime juice

Serves 8

TO MAKE CITRUS CARAMEL SAUCE:

Pound coriander, ginger, turmeric to a rough paste. Fry off in 1 tablespoon of vegetable oil until just starting to colour. Then add sugar and water. Add the rest of ingredients and bring to boil. Turn down heat and slowly reduce down to syrup consistency. Strain and cool.

TO MAKE HERB GARNISH:

Combine all ingredients in bowl and toss gently.

TO SERVE:

Place pieces of pork on serving platter, spoon over 1 tablespoon of citrus caramel per piece and garnish with herb salad.

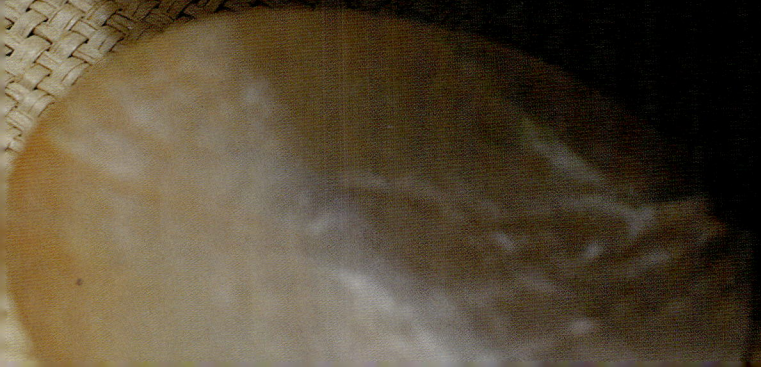

Spiced Pumpkin Soup

A fragrantly spiced soup, this is a fusion between an Australian favourite and a Thai classic.

INGREDIENTS:

1 tablespoon vegetable oil

500 ml (16 fl oz) coconut milk

1 tablespoon red curry paste

500 ml (16 fl oz) chicken stock

4 cups chopped pumpkin

2 tablespoon fish sauce

2 tablespoon palm sugar

16 green king prawns (shrimp), shelled,
   deveined, heads removed

½ cup loosely packed Thai basil

3 kaffir lime leaves, finely shredded

Serves 4

METHOD:

In saucepan, heat vegetable oil with quarter cup coconut milk. Add curry paste, stir over low heat for 5 minutes. Add the pumpkin and chicken stock, simmer until pumpkin is cooked. Puree in blender, transfer to saucepan, season with palm sugar and fish sauce. Add prawns, simmer until just cooked, about 1 minute. Stir in Thai basil and remaining coconut milk.

   Divide between 4 bowls, allowing 4 prawns per person, garnish with shredded kaffir lime leaves.

Tom Yum Goong

With its juicy prawns (shrimp), pungent chilli jam and scented citrus flavours, this most elegant soup is famous throughout Thailand.

INGREDIENTS:

1 L (1¾ pint) chicken or prawn
 (shrimp) stock

2 stalks lemon grass, outer leaves
 discarded and angle cut into 5 cm
 (2 in) pieces

4 pairs kaffir lime leaves

2 tablespoons roasted chilli paste

4 slices galangal

125 ml (4 fl oz) lime juice

100 ml (3 fl oz) fish sauce

16 peeled & deveined green king prawns
 (shrimp)

1–2 red chillies, seeded & finely chopped

coriander (cilantro) for garnish

green shallots finely sliced for garnish

serves 4

METHOD:

Put stock, lemon grass, kaffir lime leaves and galangal into saucepan. Bring to boil, reduce heat to a simmer, cook for 5 minutes. Add chilli paste, lime juice, fish sauce, cook until blended. Add prawns, simmer gently until prawns are just cooked, about 1 minute. Ladle into serving bowls, garnish with chillies, coriander and shallots.

Coconut Soup of Smoked Salmon

The restaurant variation on the classic Thai Tom Kha soup – an all time, starter menu favourite.

INGREDIENTS:

1 dried red chilli, deseeded, chopped
and soaked in hot water

1 large fresh red chilli, chopped

2 cloves garlic chopped

2 golden shallots chopped

1 pinch sea salt

1 teaspoon shrimp paste

500 ml (16 fl oz) chicken stock

500 ml (16 fl oz) coconut milk

2 stalks lemon grass, pounded

3 kaffir lime leaves, torn

2 tablespoons fish sauce

1 teaspoon palm sugar

2 tablespoons lime juice

300 g (11 oz) smoked trout or salmon (buy
at the supermarket)

Serves 4

METHOD:

In a mortar and pestle crush dried chilli, fresh chilli, garlic, shallots, salt and shrimp paste until fine paste.

Flake the smoked fish very coarsely.

In a large pot, bring stock and coconut milk to a boil, then stir in paste, simmer for a few minutes.

Add the lemon grass and lime leaves. Adjust the balance of flavours by adding the fish sauce, palm sugar and lime juice. Add the pieces of smoked fish. Heat through and serve in Chinese tea cups or small bowls.

Salads

Salad of Steamed Salmon with Yellow Bean & Ginger Dressing

Everyone's favourite fish is highlighted in this delicious Thai salad. For a smokier version, chargrill the salmon on the barbecue.

INGREDIENTS:

500 g (1 lb) Atlantic salmon, skin off, pin bones out

1 Lebanese cucumber, halved lengthways and sliced

1 punnet cherry tomatoes, halved

2 green shallots, finely sliced

1 large red chilli, seeded and julienned

½ cup coriander (cilantro) leaves

½ cup mint leaves

½ cup Yellow Bean and Ginger Dressing

1 tablespoon toasted sesame seeds

½ teaspoon roasted chilli powder

FOR YELLOW BEAN & GINGER DRESSING:

2 cloves garlic

2 medium red chillies, deseeded and chopped

½ cup ginger, finely shredded

½ cup (125 ml/4 fl oz) light soy sauce

½ cup (125 ml/4 fl oz) sweet soy sauce (kecap manis)

½ (125 ml/4 fl oz) cup coconut vinegar

⅓ cup yellow bean sauce

⅓ cup palm sugar

½ teaspoon sesame oil

Serves 4

METHOD:

Line a steamer basket with banana leaf or grease proof paper. Make a few slits in the leaf to allow the steam through. Add salmon and place basket over wok half full of simmering water. Cover and steam gently until salmon is just cooked, about 7–10 minutes. Remove from heat and cool.

When cool, break salmon into large bite size pieces and place in large mixing bowl with the cucumber, tomatoes, green shallots, chilli, coriander and mint leaves. Add yellow bean and ginger dressing. Toss gently, transfer to serving plate. Garnish with sesame seeds and chilli powder.

Yellow Bean & Ginger Dressing

This recipe makes a larger than needed quantity. It will keep in the fridge for a month and is also great for flavouring stir-fry dishes.

TO MAKE YELLOW BEAN & GINGER DRESSING:

Make a paste with the garlic and chilli, transfer to a saucepan with the remaining ingredients. Bring to the boil and simmer a few minutes until the palm sugar is dissolved. Cool and then transfer to a clean jar.

Keep in the fridge.

Salad of Sweet Pork with Green Chilli & Lime Dressing

Be warned, this sweet pork is addictive!

SWEET PORK:

500 g (1 lb) pork neck

125 g (4 oz) white sugar

2 tablespoons water

2 tablespoons fish sauce

1 tablespoon soy sauce

1 tablespoon dark soy sauce

2 star anise

DRESSING:

5 cloves garlic

2 tablespoons chopped coriander
(cilantro) root and stem

6–8 green chillies (preferably Serrano)

1 teaspoon sea salt

1 tablespoon palm sugar

3 tablespoons fish sauce

½ cup lime juice

10 red shallots, finely sliced

SALAD:

1 cup coriander (cilantro) leaves

1 cup mint leaves

2 tablespoons roasted and crushed
peanuts

2 tablespoons crispy fried shallots

Serves 4

METHOD:

Slice pork into 2.5 cm (1 in) strips, place in saucepan and cover with cold water.

Bring to the boil, remove from heat. Strain and set aside.

To caramelise sugar, place in a heavy based saucepan with 2 tablespoons of water. Stir briefly over medium heat until sugar dissolves, then boil rapidly without stirring. As sugar starts to colour around the edges, swirl the pan and keep cooking until you have obtained a rich, golden brown syrup. Immediately add fish sauce, soy sauce, dark soy sauce, and star anise, taking care not to splatter.

Add pork and simmer until tender and coated with the caramel syrup, about 10–15 minutes. Cool pork before adding to salad.

TO MAKE GREEN CHILLI & LIME DRESSING:

To make the dressing pound garlic, coriander, salt and chillies to a paste in a mortar. In a bowl, dissolve palm sugar in fish sauce, then stir in the lime juice, shallots and paste.

TO SERVE:

To assemble the salad, in a large bowl combine the coriander leaves, mint leaves and sweet pork. Toss through the dressing. Transfer to a serving platter and sprinkle with the crushed peanuts and crispy shallots.

Cuttlefish, Snake Bean & Cashew Salad with Chilli Coconut Dressing

An elegant Thai salad that can also be made with chicken or prawns (shrimp).
This dish showcases the vibrant interplay of flavours characteristic of this style of salad.

DRESSING:

1 tablespoon dark palm sugar

2 tablespoons water

75 ml (2½ fl oz) coconut cream

2 teaspoons chilli jam

2 tablespoons lime juice

1 tablespoon fish sauce

SALAD:

500 g (1 lb) cleaned and scored
   cuttlefish

2 tablespoons oyster sauce

2 tablespoons vegetable oil

¼ cup mint leaves

¼ cup coriander (cilantro) leaves

¼ cup basil leaves

3 golden shallots, finely sliced

2 tablespoons finely julienned ginger

2 large red chillies, seeded and finely
   sliced

2 stalks lemongrass, finely sliced

¼ cup roasted cashews

125 g (4 oz) snake beans, blanched,
   sliced on diagonal

1 tablespoon crispy shallots to garnish

CRISPY SHALLOTS:

500 g (1 lb) red or golden shallots,
   peeled and sliced thinly and evenly

4 cups vegetable oil

Serves 4

METHOD:

To make the dressing, combine the palm sugar and water in a small pan and stir over low heat until sugar is dissolved. Cool, then add remaining dressing ingredients.

To make the salad, toss cuttlefish with oyster sauce and leave for 1 hour. Heat half the oil in a wok until smoking, sear half the cuttlefish until just cooked—about 4–5 minutes. Transfer to a large bowl.

Heat with remaining oil and repeat process with remaining cuttlefish.

Add all remaining ingredients to bowl except the crispy shallots, toss with the dressing and transfer to serving plate. Garnish with the crispy shallots.

Crispy Shallots

A wonderful crunchy garnish for stir fries or salads, buy them in packets in Asian supermarkets or make your own.

Bottle the oil when it has cooled—it will have a lovely shallot flavour and can be used for cooking vegetables, noodles or fried rice.

TO MAKE CRISPY SHALLOTS:

Heat the oil in wok, add all the shallot slices and cook slowly on a gentle heat so that they don't burn. When shallot slices are golden brown, remove from wok with slotted spoon and drain on paper towel. Store in air tight container.

Barbecued Cuttlefish Salad with Snow Peas & Lemongrass

This dish is almost a one-bowl wonder, with a diverse mix of crisp and fresh vegetables tossed with delicious chargrilled cuttlefish. It also demonstrates how red curry paste is used in Thai cooking as a seasoning for a vast array of dishes.

INGREDIENTS:

500 g (1 lb) cleaned cuttlefish or squid

2 teaspoons rice or corn flour

2 teaspoons Shaoxing wine

2 cloves garlic, peeled and crushed

2 teaspoons ginger, grated

3 tablespoons vegetable oil

DRESSING:

2 teaspoons red curry paste

2 cloves garlic, peeled and crushed

½ cup (125 ml/4 fl oz) lime juice

½ cup (125 ml/4 fl oz) fish sauce

4 tablespoons light palm sugar

2 tablespoons roasted rice powder

SALAD:

100 g (3½ oz) baby cos lettuce leaves

½ red capsicum (sweet pepper), julienned

½ green capsicum (sweet pepper), julienned

100 g (3½ oz) snow peas (mange tout), topped, tailed and julienned

⅓ cup lemongrass, bottom half only and outer leaves removed, finely sliced

½ red onion, sliced

¼ cup mint leaves

¼ cup coriander (cilantro) leaves

2 tomatoes, cut into wedges

1 small Lebanese cucumber, sliced

Serves 6–8 as part of a selection of dishes

METHOD:

To marinate cuttlefish: Mix together the rice or corn flour, wine, garlic, ginger and oil, add cuttlefish and marinate for 2 hours.

TO MAKE DRESSING:

Mix ingredients in a bowl until the sugar is dissolved.

TO MAKE SALAD:

Heat the barbecue (grill) to hot and grill (broil) cuttlefish until just cooked. This should take about 5 minutes. Combine in a bowl with the dressing and salad ingredients. Transfer to serving plate.

Chinese New Year Salad

I have taught many variations on Chinese New Year Salad in my classes over the years. Though traditionally served at New Year, it's delicious at any time and with any Asian meal. Use your imagination as the salad is more about technique than precise ingredients—I have used many varieties of vegetables when serving this as a side dish. Beans, fresh baby corn, celery and capsicum (sweet pepper) all work well. Fresh shredded Chinese cabbage can be tossed through in the final stages along with other herbs like mint, basil or Vietnamese mint. If you like some bite, add fresh red or green chillies.

INGREDIENTS:

½ cup (125 ml/4 fl oz) rice or coconut vinegar

½ cup (125 ml/4 fl oz) water

1 cup (250 g/8 oz) white sugar

1 teaspoon salt

1 cup carrot, shredded

1 cup white radish, shredded

1 cup cucumber, shredded

1 small red onion, thinly sliced

2 tablespoons ginger, finely shredded

1 cup bean sprouts, topped and tailed

8 kaffir lime leaves, centre rib removed and finely shredded

½ cup coriander (cilantro) leaves

½ cup mint leaves

1 tablespoon toasted sesame seeds

DRESSING:

2 tablespoon Chinese plum sauce

2 teaspoon white sugar

pinch of salt

2 tablespoons warm water

2 tablespoons lime juice

1 teaspoon sesame oil

Serves 6-8 as part of a selection of dishes

METHOD:

Combine the vinegar, water, sugar and teaspoon of salt in a saucepan and bring to the boil, stirring occasionally. When the sugar has dissolved, remove from heat and cool.

In a bowl, mix together the carrot, radish, cucumber, onion and ginger. Pour over the cooled vinegar syrup and allow to pickle for at least 2 hours. This can be done the day before and refrigerated until needed.

Drain the pickled vegetables from the liquid and transfer to a bowl along with the bean sprouts, kaffir lime leaves, coriander and mint leaves. Pour over the dressing and mix to combine, transfer to a serving plate and sprinkle with the sesame seeds.

MAKE THE DRESSING:

Combine all ingredients in a bowl and whisk together.

Glass Noodle Salad with Chicken & Prawns

Glass noodles are made from mung bean starch, and are often labelled 'vermicelli'. They turn transparent when soaked and have little taste, but are used for their bouncy texture and ability to soak up other flavours. Vermicelli noodles can also be made from rice flour, but these have a different texture and tend to go mushy if overcooked. To make sure you have the correct noodles for this dish, just read the list of ingredients on the packet and look for green beans or mung beans, not rice.

INGREDIENTS:

125 g (4 oz) glass noodles, soaked in boiling water until soft and translucent (about 10 minutes), then drained

6–8 large cooked prawns (shrimp), peeled and de-veined and cut into bite-sized pieces

250 g (8 oz) cooked chicken meat, cut into bite-sized pieces

2 stalks lemongrass, bottom half only and outer leaves discarded, very thinly sliced

2 spring onions (scallions), thinly sliced including some of the green top

2–4 small red chillies, or 1 large, finely chopped (de-seed if mild preferred)

½ cup mint leaves

½ cup coriander (cilantro) leaves

½ baby cos lettuce, finely shredded

1 tablespoon Crispy Golden Shallots (see page 44)

DRESSING:

6 tablespoons lime juice

2 tablespoons fish sauce

1 tablespoon roasted chilli paste

1 tablespoon light palm sugar

Serves 6–8 as part of a selection of dishes

METHOD:

To assemble salad: In a large bowl, toss the noodles, prawns, chicken, lemongrass, spring onions, chillies, mint and coriander. Add the dressing and toss to combine.

Line serving plate or bowl with the shredded lettuce and mound the noodle salad on top. Garnish with the Crispy Golden Shallots.

TO MAKE DRESSING:

Combine all dressing ingredients in a bowl and stir to dissolve sugar.

Seafood Salad from Krabi

I had this simple salad at a rustic cafe in Southern Thailand a few years ago. It has always stayed in my mind because of the attention to detail. The squid and prawns (shrimp) had been bought at the market that morning. The seafood was quickly blanched and tossed with a handful of herbs and chillies. But what I really remember is that I could still smell the perfume in the lime juice, as it had been freshly squeezed minutes before coming out to my table. Easy to recreate at home—just open a cold Singha beer and you could be on holiday in Krabi.

This simple salad can be made more complex with the addition of finely chopped lemongrass, shredded kaffir lime leaves or chopped Chinese celery, and the dressing could be given more depth with the addition of a few cleaned and scraped coriander (cilantro) roots.

INGREDIENTS:

250 g (8 oz) green prawn (shrimp) meat
250 g (8 oz) squid, cleaned and scored
4 small green birdseye chillies (use larger de-seeded (pitted) chillies if mild is preferred)
2 cloves garlic, peeled
¼ cup (60 ml/2 fl oz) lime juice
2–3 tablespoons fish sauce
pinch of white sugar
¼ cup mint leaves
¼ cup coriander (cilantro) leaves
2 tablespoons golden shallots, thinly sliced (if unavailable use red onion)
1 medium red chilli, thinly sliced
lettuce for serving

Serves 6–8 as part of a selection of dishes

METHOD:

Bring a large pot of water to the boil, add a few teaspoons of salt and quickly blanch the prawns. They will only take about 30 seconds. Bring the water back to the boil and add the squid, removing when it has curled and become opaque. This will only take about 15 seconds. Place seafood in a bowl and toss with the dressing, herbs, shallots and red chilli. Line the serving plate with lettuce and transfer salad to the plate.

TO MAKE THE DRESSING:

Make a rough paste in a mortar and pestle with the green chillies and garlic, add the lime juice and fish sauce. Season with a pinch or two of sugar. The dressing should be hot, sour and salty.

Wok

Satay Beef with Pumpkin & Kaffir Lime Leaf

Although beef isn't a traditional stir-fry meat in Asia, this recipe uses eye fillet and is one of the most popular stir-fry dishes from our classes. Beef has a tendency to lose a lot of juice during the stir-frying process which tends to 'stew' the meat and vegetables. To avoid ending up with a stewed mess, stir-fry the beef first, set aside and keep warm, then add back into the wok just before serving.

INGREDIENTS:

1 tablespoon vegetable oil

500 g (1 lb) eye fillet, sirloin or other
   tender cut, sliced into stir-fry strips

2 cups of lightly steamed pumpkin, cut
   into 5 cms (2 in) dice

100 g (3½ oz) snow peas (mange tout),
   sliced

1 tablespoon red curry paste

¼ cup coconut cream

1 tablespoon fish sauce

1 tablespoon kecap manis (sweet
   soy sauce)

2 tablespoons roasted crushed peanuts

1 tablespoon kaffir lime leaves, shredded
   finely

Serves 4

METHOD:

Heat oil in wok until smoking, add beef and stir-fry until brown. Add curry paste, stir-fry for a few minutes until fragrant. Add coconut cream, fish sauce, kecap manis, pumpkin, snow peas and stir-fry until heated through.

   Transfer to serving plate, sprinkle with peanuts and kaffir lime leaf. Serve with steamed jasmine rice.

Stir-Fry of Pork with Pineapple, Ginger & Yellow Bean Sauce

The tartness of the pineapple blends with the mild sweet flavours of the pork—a sweet and sour stir-fry.

INGREDIENTS:

2 tablespoons vegetable oil

1 tablespoon chopped fresh garlic

2 tablespoon finely shredded ginger

500 g (1 lb) of pork fillet, sliced into stir-fry
    strips

2 tablespoons yellow bean sauce

2 tablespoons oyster sauce

2 tablespoons palm sugar

1 red capsicum (sweet pepper) cut
    into thin strips

½ fresh pineapple, peeled, cored and
    cut into chunks

½ teaspoon freshly ground white
    peppercorns

3 green shallots, thinly sliced on the
    diagonal

Serves 4

METHOD:

Heat oil in wok until moderate heat. Stir-fry garlic briefly until golden. Turn heat to high. Add pork and ginger, stir-fry until starts to colour. Add yellow bean sauce, oyster sauce, palm sugar and stir-fry until pork is cooked. Add capsicum and pineapple, stir-fry for one minute. Add white pepper and shallots, toss briefly. Transfer to serving platter, serve with steamed jasmine rice.

Stir-Fried Chinese Broccoli with Straw Mushrooms & Oyster Sauce

A popular vegetable side dish, straw mushrooms are difficult to buy fresh, but the tinned ones are suitable to use. They are also named 'paddy straw mushrooms' after their growing environment, and are one of Asia's most important mushrooms because of their very high protein content.

INGREDIENTS:

500 g (1 lb) Chinese broccoli, washed and
  trimmed
2 tablespoons vegetable oil
4 cloves garlic, chopped
1 green chilli, chopped
½ cup drained canned straw mushrooms
2 tablespoons water
2 tablespoons oyster sauce
1 tablespoon fish sauce
1 teaspoon sugar
ground white pepper to taste

Serves 4 as a side dish

METHOD:

Heat oil in a wok to moderate temperature. Add the garlic and cook briefly until just starting to colour.

Turn the heat to high, add the broccoli, chillies and mushrooms and stirfry until vegetables are starting to wilt.

Add the oyster sauce, water, fish sauce, sugar and pepper and stir-fry to combine.

Transfer to serving plate and serve at once as a vegetable side dish.

Asparagus Tossed with Prawns, Roasted Chilli Paste, Coconut Cream & Crispy Shallots

This is another simple stir-fry highlighting the versatility of roasted chilli paste. Like all recipes, you can make it your own and use chicken or pork instead of prawns (shrimp). Substitute asparagus for any other quick-cooking green vegetable. The key ingredient in this dish is roasted chilli paste.

INGREDIENTS:

½ cup (120 ml/4 fl oz) vegetable oil

¼ cup golden shallots, peeled and thinly sliced

2 cloves garlic, peeled and crushed

1 large red chilli, de-seeded (pitted) and sliced

250 g (8 oz) green prawn (shrimp) meat

1 bunch of asparagus, trimmed and ends peeled, then sliced on the diagonal into 5 cm (2 in) pieces

1 tablespoon roasted chilli paste

2 tablespoons coconut cream

2 tablespoons fish sauce

2 tablespoons lime or lemon juice

2 tablespoons water

1 tablespoon light palm sugar

2 tablespoons roasted and crushed peanuts

Serves 4

METHOD:

In a wok, heat the oil and fry the shallots until golden. Remove with a slotted spoon, drain on paper towel and set aside.

(The leftover oil can be re-used for stir fries or dressings, imparting a rich burst of roasted shallot flavour to the dish)

Drain all but 1 tablespoon of the oil, reheat in the wok and fry the garlic and chilli for a minute or so. Now add the prawns and stir-fry until they are just starting to colour. Add the asparagus and stir-fry briefly. Mix in the roasted chilli paste, coconut cream, fish sauce, lime juice, water and sugar. Cook until combined, then stir in the peanuts.

Transfer to a serving platter and garnish with Crispy Shallots (see page 44).

Sweet & Sour Chicken Omelette

Eggs play such an important part in the daily diet of Asians. Since most rural houses raise hens and ducks, eggs are readily available and provide a cheap reliable source of protein. This delicious omelette will become a family favourite. Serve with steamed jasmine rice.

FILLING:

2 tablespoons vegetable oil

5 mashed cloves of garlic

250 g (8 oz) finely chopped chicken thigh

1 tablespoon oyster sauce

1 tablespoon fish sauce

¼ cup palm sugar

3 large tomatoes, cut in half and finely sliced

1 onion, cut in half and thinly sliced

1 red capsicum (sweet pepper), finely chopped

OMELETTES:

6 tablespoons vegetable oil

8 large eggs, lightly beaten

sprigs of coriander (cilantro) for garnish

Serves 4

METHOD:

Heat oil in wok. Add garlic, sitr fry until golden. Add onion and stir-fry until softened.

Add the chicken meat, stir-fry until coloured. Add oyster sauce, fish sauce, tomatoes, capsicum and palm sugar. Simmer for 10–15 minutes. The sauce should be rather liquid. Set aside.

TO MAKE OMELETTE:

Heat oil in wok then add half of beaten eggs.

Let the eggs set for about 10 seconds then slowly rotate wok to distribute eggs in large circle. Cook until omelette is set, about 1–2 minutes.

Spoon half of filling into centre, fold omelette over the filling. Cook briefly, about 15–30 seconds. Using a spatula, slide the finished omelette onto an ovenproof platter and keep warm in a low oven. Repeat with remaining egg mix.

Garnish with coriander. Serve with steamed jasmine rice.

Crispy Fish Stir-Fried with Curry Paste, Wild Ginger & Green Peppercorns

To simplify this dish, the deep-fried fish pieces can be substituted with stir-fried strips of chicken, pork or beef. Prawns (shrimp) and squid also make a great alternative.

Krachai is a variety of ginger referred to in English as 'wild ginger'. It has a distinctive earthy flavour with a musk-like perfume. Both krachai and green peppercorns are difficult to source fresh, but the imported pickled versions from Thailand make a great substitute. They can be left out, but if you want to expand your knowledge of Thai cuisine, they're worth using as both are very common ingredients in stir fries and curries.

INGREDIENTS:

350 g (12½ oz) good quality fresh fish, cut on the diagonal into thin medallions
corn or rice flour for dusting
2 cups (500 ml/17 fl oz) vegetable oil for deep-frying
2 extra tablespoons vegetable oil
2 tablespoons red curry paste
1–2 tablespoons light palm sugar
1–2 tablespoons fish sauce
1–2 tablespoons water
1 tablespoon shredded krachai, fresh or pickled, rinsed of brine
1 tablespoon pickled green peppercorns, rinsed of brine
10 kaffir lime leaves
½ cup basil leaves

Serves 6–8 as part of a selection of dishes

METHOD:

Toss the fish pieces in the rice or corn flour. Heat the oil in a wok to a medium heat. Deep-fry the fish in batches until crispy and golden. If the fish has been cut thinly, this should only take 3–4 minutes. Drain on paper towel and repeat until all the fish is cooked.

Drain oil from wok and set aside. Wipe out the wok, add the extra oil and heat to moderate before adding the red curry paste. Fry gently until fragrant, then add the palm sugar, fish sauce and water. Bring to the boil and simmer until palm sugar has dissolved. Add the krachai, green peppercorns and kaffir lime leaves. Simmer a few minutes and then toss through all the fish.

Lastly, add the basil and as soon as the leaves wilt, remove from the heat.

Singapore-Style Seafood Noodles

Another classic noodle dish that has found its way throughout South-East Asia. I love the combination of chewy Hokkien noodles and bouncy rice vermicelli with the rustic and hearty seafood sauce.

INGREDIENTS:

2 tablespoons vegetable oil

3 cloves garlic, peeled and crushed

1 small golden shallot, peeled and sliced

50 g (1¾ oz) finely chopped pork fillet

50 g (1¾ oz) green prawn (shrimp) meat

50 g (1¾ oz) squid, cleaned and sliced

1 egg

1 tablespoon soy sauce

1 tablespoon fish sauce

pinch of white sugar

30 g (1 oz) rice vermicelli noodles, soaked
    in hot water until softened, then drained

60g (2 oz) fresh Hokkien noodles

1–2 tablespoons chicken stock or water

pinch of white pepper

¼ cup bean sprouts

a few garlic chives or green spring onions
    (scallions), sliced

½ large red chilli, sliced

lime wedge to garnish

Serves 1–2

METHOD:

Heat oil to moderate and stir-fry the garlic and shallot until just starting to colour. Add the pork and stir-fry a few minutes, then add the prawn and squid and keep stir-frying for another minute or so. Push to the side of the wok and break in the egg. Scramble briefly and then add the soy sauce, fish sauce and sugar. Stir everything together and then add all the noodles. Add the stock or water and keep cooking until the noodles have softened.

Stir in the white pepper, bean sprouts and garlic chives. Transfer to a serving plate and garnish with chilli and lime wedges.

Chicken Stir-Fried with Black Beans, Ginger & Lime

An easy family friendly, chicken stir-fry using the classic combination of salty black beans and ginger.

INGREDIENTS:

2 tablespoons vegetable oil

500 g (1 lb) sliced chicken breast or
thigh meat

3–4 tablespoons black bean sauce

1 lime, cut into thin slices

1 red capsicum (sweet pepper), cut into
stir-fry strips

125 g (4½ oz) snow peas (mange tout),
trimmed

4 green shallots, sliced thinly on the
diagonal

Serves 4

TO MAKE THE SAUCE:

Soak the black beans in ½ cup of hot water for 10 minutes. Drain (reserve the soaking water).

Heat the vegetable oil to moderate and fry the ginger, garlic and chilli.

Add the black beans, soy sauce, sugar and pepper and enough of the soaking water to make a thick sauce.

This sauce will keep for a month in the refrigerator.

TO COOK THE CHICKEN:

Heat the oil until very hot and stir-fry the chicken until almost cooked.

Add the black bean sauce and stir-fry briefly before adding the lime slices, capsicum, snow peas and green shallots.

Stir-fry to combine and then transfer to serving plates or platter.

Beef Stir-Fried with Oyster Sauce, Broccoli & Pickled Ginger

The origins of this classic stir-fry are certainly Chinese but the Thais, with their usual culinary confidence, have tweaked the dish and added the characteristic flavour of fish sauce. It's usually served with a vinegar and chilli condiment to liven things up.

The condiment is so easy to make and is one of the condiments—along with chilli powder, sugar and fish sauce—found on just about every Thai table. It allows the individual diner to adjust the hot, sour, sweet and salty flavours that are keynotes in Thai food.

Do be bold and use small chillies as they have more intense floral notes compared to larger chillies which are more capsicum (sweet pepper)-like in flavour. A great chilli that has a medium punch and brilliant taste is the Serrano, which can often be found in large supermarkets. The pickled ginger can be bought in most big supermarkets or just use a tablespoon of shredded fresh ginger and add with the garlic.

Like all stir-fries, don't overload the wok with too much meat or too many vegetables. Other vegetables such as broccolini, cauliflower, asparagus or snow peas (mange tout) work just as well as the broccoli.

INGREDIENTS:

2 tablespoons vegetable oil

400 g (14 oz) sliced beef rump or fillet

1 small brown onion, thinly sliced

2 cloves garlic, peeled and minced (ground)

2 tablespoons oyster sauce

2 tablespoons fish sauce

2 tablespoons light palm sugar

1–2 tablespoons water

2 cups broccoli florets

2 tablespoons pickled ginger, shredded

CHILLI VINEGAR CONDIMENT (PHRIK DONG NAM SOM)

½ cup (125 ml/4 fl oz) rice or coconut vinegar

1 tablespoon fish sauce

2–10 small, hot red and green chillies

Serves 4 or 6–8 as part of a selection of dishes

TO MAKE STIR-FRY:

Heat the oil in a wok to smoking, add the beef and stir-fry for a minute to seal. Add the onion and garlic. Stir-fry another minute. Add the oyster sauce, fish sauce, palm sugar and water and keep stir-frying for the sauces to combine. Now add the broccoli and stir-fry briefly. Mix through the pickled ginger and transfer to a serving plate. Serve with Chilli Vinegar Condiment.

TO MAKE CONDIMENT:

Slice chillies and add to a small bowl with the vinegar and fish sauce.

Curries

Red Curry Paste

Red is the most versatile of Thai curry pastes, used in fish cakes, satays, marinades, stir-fries, as well as curries. A red curry paste is usually made from dried red chillies, rather than fresh ones. This paste keeps for 2–3 weeks in a tightly sealed glass jar in the refrigerator, or store in the freezer for up to 6 months in ice cube trays and thaw cubes as required.

INGREDIENTS:

15 dried medium red chillies, soaked in hot water until soft, about 10 minutes, then drained and chopped finely

2 teaspoons coriander (cilantro) seeds

1 teaspoon cumin seeds

½ teaspoon mace

2 teaspoons white peppercorns

2 small red shallots, peeled

12 cloves garlic, peeled

2 stalks lemongrass, finely sliced

1 tablespoon galangal, chopped

2 tablespoons coriander (cilantro) root, chopped

1 tablespoon lime zest

2 teaspoons salt

2 teaspoons shrimp paste, roasted

Makes 2 cups

METHOD:

Combine coriander seeds, cumin and mace in a small frying pan and toast over a moderate heat until aromatic—this will take about 3 minutes. Grind this mixture with the white peppercorns in a mortar with a pestle. Add remaining ingredients and pound until you have obtained a smooth paste

Perfect Rice

The first thing every young Thai girl learns is how to cook rice, because if she can cook rice, she can make a meal. Long-grained jasmine rice is the preferred rice for most Thais, except those from the north and north-east who prefer sticky rice.

INGREDIENTS:
2 cups jasmine rice
3 cups (750 ml/26 fl oz) cold water

Serves 4

METHOD:
Wash the rice in several changes of water until the water is fairly clear. Drain well and place in a saucepan or rice cooker.

Cover with water up to the first joint on the index finger. (I used to be sceptical about the knuckle technique, but it is a reliable method.) Don't add salt to the water. Jasmine rice has its own delicate perfume which is destroyed by salt.

If using a saucepan, cover with a lid and bring water to the boil. Reduce heat to low and cook rice without stirring for about 15–20 minutes. Lift the lid to check that it is cooked, cook for 1–2 minutes longer if necessary. The rice is done when the grains are soft enough to crush between your thumb and forefinger. Turn off the heat and let the rice stand covered for 8–10 minutes to absorb the steam before serving.

Sometimes the top of the rice can be a little dry at the end of cooking, as it varies in its ability to absorb water depending on the growing conditions. Just sprinkle on some more water and cook a few more minutes.

Penang style Chicken Curry with Green Peppercorns & Pumpkin

This moderately hot curry, always containing peanuts, originated in Penang, an island in the Malacca Straits just south of Thailand. The whole green peppercorns add a burst of heat.

INGREDIENTS:

500 g (1 lb) chicken thigh meat, cut into bite size pieces

2 teaspoons fresh or tinned green peppercorns

2 cups lightly steamed pumpkin pieces

2 tablespoons vegetable oil

½ cup coconut cream

¼ cup red curry paste

400 ml (12 fl oz) coconut milk

2 tablespoons palm sugar

3 tablespoons fish sauce

½ cup roasted, crushed peanuts

1 cup of loosely packed Thai Basil leaves

Serves 4

METHOD:

Rub chicken pieces with crushed peppercorns. Combine vegetable oil and coconut cream in wok. Heat until sizzling, stirring constantly. Add curry paste and cook, stirring until fragrant, about 5 minutes. Add chicken and stir until sealed.

Add coconut milk, sugar, fish sauce, peanuts and bring to the boil, stirring well.

Add pumpkin pieces, simmer until well coated with the sauce and cooked through.

Add basil leaves, stir until wilted. Transfer to serving plate.

Green Curry of Sword Fish With Bamboo Shoots & Ginger

Green curry is one of the most known and loved of all Thai curries. This curry requires some work but is well worth the effort. Left over paste can be frozen for six months. This curry is equally delicious with any other seafood, meat or poultry.

GREEN CURRY PASTE:

1 tablespoon coriander (cilantro) seed, roasted

1 teaspoon cumin, roasted

1 teaspoon mace

1 teaspoon white pepper, ground

½ cup chopped onion or golden shallots

6 cloves garlic

1 tablespoon chopped galangal

2 stalks lemon grass, bottom half only, finely chopped

5 large green chillies, seeded and chopped

6 small green chillies, chopped

4 coriander (cilantro) roots, cleaned, scraped and chopped

1 tablespoon krachai

1 tablespoon fresh turmeric, peeled and chopped

1 tablespoon lime zest

1 tablespoon shrimp paste, roasted

1 teaspoon salt

CURRY:

500 ml (16 fl oz) coconut cream

3 tablespoons vegetable oil

4 tablespoons green curry paste

2 tablespoons finely shredded ginger

4 double kaffir lime leaves

2 large green chillies, seeded and sliced

3 tablespoons fish sauce

3 tablespoons light palm sugar

2 tablespoons tamarind water

500 g (1 lb) swordfish, cut into 3–4 cm (2 inch) pieces

½ cup bamboo shoots

1 punnet of baby corn

½ cup lemon basil

Serves 4-6

TO MAKE GREEN CURRY PASTE:

Combine the spices in a mortar and pestle and grind finely.

Add the remaining ingredients and pound to a paste.

TO MAKE CURRY:

Remove 3 tablespoons of coconut cream from the top of the tin of coconut. Combine in a wok with the vegetable oil and cook over a low heat until the oil is released from the coconut cream. Add the paste and fry gently for 5 minutes.

Add the ginger, kaffir lime leaves, green chillies, fish sauce and palm sugar. Stir for a minute to combine and then add the remaining coconut cream and tamarind water. Bring to the boil and then add the swordfish, bamboo shoots and baby corn.

Simmer for 3 minutes, stir in basil. Transfer to serving bowl. Serve with steamed jasmine rice.

Hang Lae Pork Curry with Cassia & Star Anise

This curry is as famous in the north as Massaman is in the south. It doesn't contain coconut milk but is as rich and unctuous from the slow braising of the pork. Redolent with sweet spices like star anise and cinnamon, deeply aromatic from the generous use of ginger and pickled garlic.

Thai pickled garlic is available in jars from Asian supermarkets. It is preserved in a sweet, sour salty brine and tastes like a cross between roasted garlic and pickled onion.

This recipe makes a generous quantity—any leftovers freeze well.

FOR THE PORK:

1 kg (2.2 lb) pork belly
1 kg (2.2 lb) pork neck
350 g hang lae curry paste

FOR THE HANG LAE CURRY PASTE:

10 dried long red chillies, deseeded, soaked and drained
large pinch salt
1 tablespoon galangal, chopped
6 tablespoons lemongrass, chopped
2 tablespoons ginger, chopped
1 tablespoon red turmeric, chopped
8 tablespoons red shallots, chopped
6 tablespoons garlic, chopped
1 tablespoon coriander (cilantro) seeds, roasted and ground
½ tablespoon cumin seeds, roasted and ground
3 star anise, roasted and ground
2 cm (¾ in) cassia bark, roasted and ground
5 cloves, roasted and ground
2 cardamon pods, roasted and ground

FOR THE CURRY:

½ cup vegetable oil
½ cup palm sugar
½ cup fish sauce
3 tablespoons tamarind water
chicken stock or water
20 red shallots, peeled
2 cups coarsely shredded ginger
1 cup pickled garlic, peeled
a little pickled garlic syrup
½ cup peanuts

TO MAKE THE CURRY PASTE:

Make a somewhat coarse paste by pounding the ingredients in a mortar and pestle,

TO PREPARE THE PORK:

Cut the pork belly and neck into approx. 2 cm x 2 cm pieces. Marinade the pork in the curry paste for no less than 2 hours.

TO MAKE THE CURRY:

Heat vegetable oil and fry the pork, stirring regularly to prevent burning, until the pork is brown.

Season with the sugar, fish sauce and tamarind water. Moisten with the stock or water to just cover. Add the whole shallots, shredded ginger, pickled garlic, pickled garlic syrup and peanuts. Simmer uncovered until pork is tender, about 2 hours.

Check seasoning: it should be salty, aromatic, smoky, spicy and a little sweet and sour, with flavors of ginger and star anise. There should be a nice amount of oil dappled across the surface of the curry.

Pork Curry with Water Spinach, Kaffir Lime & Tamarind

This is a very easy and light style of red curry. Use baby spinach or Asian greens if water spinach is unavailable. Kaffir lime juice, with its intense perfume, is traditionally used to finish but ordinary limes will be fine.

INGREDIENTS

3 tablespoons vegetable oil

3 cloves garlic, peeled and finely sliced

2 tablespoons red curry paste

250 ml (8 fl oz) coconut milk

400 g (14 oz) pork fillet, cut into strips

8 kaffir lime leaves

2 tablespoons fish sauce

2 tablespoons soy sauce

2 tablespoons tamarind water

1 tablespoon light palm sugar

250 ml (8 fl oz) chicken stock or water

125 g (4 oz) water spinach, English
  spinach or other leafy green

lime juice to taste

Serves 4 or 6–8 as part of a selection of dishes

METHOD:

Heat the oil to moderate and fry the garlic, taking care not to burn it. Add the curry paste and fry until fragrant. Add the coconut milk and bring to the boil. Reduce to a simmer and add the pork fillet, lime leaves, fish sauce, soy sauce, tamarind water and palm sugar. Allow to simmer, stirring until the pork has cooked. This will only take a few minutes. Add the chicken stock and water spinach and simmer a further few minutes until the spinach has wilted. Add a squeeze of lime juice to taste and transfer to a serving bowl.

Southern Style Chicken Curry with Turmeric & Potatoes

The name of this dish, Gai Kolae, refers to the fishing boats found in the waters of southern Thailand. Like the boats, it has a vibrant colour from the fresh turmeric and fresh red and green chillies.

CURRY PASTE:

5 large dried chillies, de-seeded (pitted) and soaked in hot water for 10 minutes

pinch of salt

1 teaspoon fresh turmeric, peeled and roughly chopped

1 teaspoon coriander (cilantro) seeds, roasted and ground

1 teaspoon cumin seeds, roasted and ground

1 teaspoon roasted shrimp paste

CURRY:

4 tablespoons vegetable oil

4 skinless chicken Maryland, cut at the joint and cut in half again

1 tablespoon garlic, roughly chopped

500 ml (16 fl oz) coconut milk

250 ml (8 fl oz) chicken stock or water

4 tablespoons fish sauce

2 tablespoons light palm sugar

300 g (11 oz) peeled waxy potatoes, cut into chunks

1 large red chilli, de-seeded (pitted) and sliced

1 large green chilli, de-seeded (pitted) and sliced lime juice to taste

coriander (cilantro) sprigs to garnish

Serves 4 or 6–8 as part of a selection of dishes

TO MAKE CURRY PASTE:

Finely chop the chillies, add to a mortar with the remaining ingredients and pound to a smooth paste with a pestle.

TO MAKE CURRY:

Heat the oil in a wok or saucepan and fry the chicken pieces until golden. Remove and then fry the garlic on a moderate heat until starting to colour. Add all the curry paste and fry gently until fragrant.

Add the coconut milk, stock, chicken, fish sauce and palm sugar. Bring to the boil then simmer for 15–20 minutes.

Add the potatoes and simmer until tender. Finish with the lime juice and chillies, transfer to a serving bowl and garnish with the coriander.

Steamed Red Curry with Prawns & Pumpkin

Hor Mok Pla is a steamed fish curry that can often be found at curry vendors throughout Thailand. I like to do an elegant version in the class, where we line a bamboo steamer basket with banana leaves, add a layer of basil, a layer of seafood and then pour the curry sauce over the seafood before gently steaming. The basket is placed on the table with the other dishes and shared. It's a sublime, delicate and creamy curry—perfect for an impressive Thai dinner party. The following version uses the combination of prawns (shrimp) and pumpkin but you could also use a mix of seafood, or omit the pumpkin altogether. Like so many recipes, this is about the technique.

If you don't have banana leaves on hand, baking paper is fine; and another alternative is just to steam the dish in a glass or porcelain bowl. It could also be divided between small bowls and served as an entree or starter. The steaming time will vary slightly depending on the size of the basket or bowl.

CURRY SAUCE:

2 cups (500 ml/17 fl oz) coconut cream

2 tablespoons light palm sugar

2 tablespoons fish sauce

2 eggs, lightly beaten

2–3 tablespoons red curry paste

CURRY:

1 cup basil leaves

16 large green prawns (shrimp), peeled, de-veined, heads and tails removed

2 cups Kent pumpkin, peeled, cut into 5 cm (2 in) pieces and lightly steamed

8 kaffir lime leaves, finely shredded

curry sauce

½ large red chilli, de-seeded (pitted) and cut into fine shreds

handful of coriander (cilantro) leaves for garnish

Serves 4–8 as part of a selection of dishes

TO MAKE CURRY SAUCE:

Open the coconut cream without shaking it and remove thick cream from the top. Reserve cream for garnish. Combine the palm sugar and fish sauce in a bowl, stir to dissolve palm sugar, add the eggs, curry paste and coconut cream.

TO MAKE CURRY:

Line a medium steamer basket with banana leaves or baking paper. Layer over the basil leaves, then the prawns and pumpkin. Sprinkle over half the shredded kaffir lime leaves and then the curry sauce. Place basket over a wok filled with boiling water. Cover and steam over a moderate heat for about 15–20 minutes. Remove from heat and place basket on a serving plate. Swirl over reserved coconut cream, reserved kaffir lime leaves, chilli strips and coriander leaves.

Indonesian Beef Rendang

Originally from West Sumatra, this caramelised beef curry was served for ceremonial occasions to honour guests. Now popular throughout Indonesia and Malaysia, like other slow braised dishes, it is easy to make in large quantities. Rendang has been voted Number One in the world's 50 most delicious foods.

FOR THE RENDANG PASTE:

2½ tablespoons black pepper

2½ tablespoons coriander (cilantro) seeds, roasted and ground

50 g (1¾ oz) ginger

50 g (2 oz) galangal

250 g (8½) large red chillies, seeded and chopped

40 g (1½ oz) birds eye chillies, finely chopped

50 g (1¾ oz) garlic

200 g (7 oz) shallots

100 g (3½ oz) candlenuts (or substitute with macadamia nuts)

FOR THE RENDANG:

2 tablespoons vegetable oil

½ cup rendang paste

750 g (1.5 lb) chuck beef, cut into 2.5 cm (1 in) cubes

2 stalks lemongrass

1 turmeric leaf (if available)

4 slices galangal

1 cup water

500 ml (16 fl oz) coconut cream

2 tablespoons dark palm sugar

⅓ cup sweet soy sauce

Serves 4

TO MAKE THE CURRY PASTE:

Pound the spices, ginger and galangal in a mortar and pestle then add the rest of the ingredients and pound to form a coarse paste.

TO MAKE THE RENDANG:

Heat the oil in a heavy based pan or pot and fry the paste for 2–3 minutes. Add the meat, lemongrass, turmeric leaf and galangal and cook until the meat is sealed all over. Add the water and simmer gently for 40 minutes. Add the coconut cream, palm sugar and kecap manis. Simmer for another 45–60 minutes until the meat is tender and the sauce is very thick. Serve in bowls with steamed rice.

Chargrill

Black Pepper Prawns with Chargrilled Pineapple

A fantastic recipe for your next barbecue which showcases the abundant local fresh produce available to the Spirit House chefs.

INGREDIENTS:

1½ teaspoons whole black peppercorns

4 cloves peeled garlic

1 tablespoon ginger, peeled and roughly chopped

2 tablespoons vegetable oil i.e., grape seed, sunflower, safflower

3 spring onions (scallions), thinly slice bottom half and shred green tops for garnish

1 tablespoon fermented black beans, rinsed and drained

3 tablespoons kecap manis (sweet soy sauce)

1 tablespoon thin or light soy sauce

1½ tablespoons dark palm sugar

1 tablespoon lime juice

half pineapple, peeled, sliced in half lengthways and cut into 5 mm slices

12 large prawns (shrimp), peeled, deveined but leave the heads on

1 large red chilli, thinly sliced on the angle for garnish.

Serves 4

BLACK PEPPER SAUCE METHOD:

Crush the peppercorns in a mortar, add the garlic and ginger and pound to a paste.

Heat the oil in a saucepan to moderate heat and gently fry the paste and bottom half of the spring onions for a minute or so. Add the black beans, kecap manis, soy sauce and palm sugar and bring to a simmer, cooking until the sugar has dissolved. Remove from heat and stir in lime juice.

PRAWNS METHOD:

Heat the barbecue to medium and brush with vegetable oil.

Grill pineapple until warmed through and slightly charred.

Cook prawns taking care not to overcook. They should take about 5–7 minutes depending on their size.

TO SERVE:

Transfer to a serving plate with the grilled pineapple, spoon over the black pepper sauce and garnish with shredded spring onions and sliced red chilli.

Grilled Beef Ribs with Orange, Mint & Cherry Tomato Salad

Spirit House chefs chargrilled over 500 portions of these delicious ribs at a recent Noosa Food & Wine Festival. For a simple variation, serve the fragrant salad with some barbecued beef or pork fillet that has been brushed with a few tablespoons of Kecap manis (sweet soy sauce).

FOR THE BRAISE:

1 lt (32 fl oz) coconut cream

2 lt (64 fl oz) chicken stock

5 lime leaves

1 stem lemon grass

100 g (3½ oz) ginger

FOR THE SWEET CHILLI DRESSING:

100 ml (2¾ fl oz) sweet chilli sauce

50 ml (1¾ fl oz) lime juice

fish sauce to taste

FOR THE RIBS:

3 kg (6 lb/10oz) braised beef ribs

50 ml (1¾ fl oz) sweet soy sauce

50 ml (1¾ fl oz) vegetable oil

1 tablespoon salt

FOR THE SALAD:

2 cups coriander (cilantro) leaves only

2 cups mint, leaves only

1 medium red onion, thinly sliced

2 oranges, segmented

1 punnet cherry tomatoes, cut in half

2 tablespoons roasted sesame seeds

2 large red chillies, deseeded, julienned

6 kaffir lime leaves, shredded

half cup ginger, julienned

2 sticks lemongrass, trimmed and thinly sliced

250 ml (8fl oz) sweet chilli dressing

BRAISE METHOD:

On barbecue, char the ribs on the outside to seal the meat. In a pot bring to boil the rest of the ingredients. Place ribs in a tray and pour liquid mixture on top. Cover tray with foil and place in a preheated oven at 175°C (325°F/Gas Mark 3) for 2½ hours. Check to see if ribs are tender at this time. They may need another 30 minutes. Take out of tray and cool down for 2 hours before grilling.

SWEET CHILLI DRESSING METHOD:

Combine sweet chilli sauce and lime juice in a bowl and mix together. Add the fish sauce a little at a time, tasting as you go. It should taste sweet, sour and a little salty.

GRILLED BEEF RIBS METHOD:

Preheat barbecue to medium heat. In a bowl, place ribs and coat with sweet soy, oil and salt. Place ribs on barbecue and slowly grill, turning every so often to char all over.

SALAD METHOD:

In another bowl, add coriander, mint, orange segments, onion, cherry tomatoes, half the sesame seeds, chilli, lime leaves, ginger and lemongrass. Mix well, then toss with some of the sweet chilli dressing.

TO SERVE:

On a platter, place ribs and dress with leftover dressing. Gently place salad all over the ribs and sprinkle the rest of the sesame seeds over the top, then serve.

Serves 4

Soy Glazed Salmon with Avocado, Sesame & Mirin Dressing

Inspired by fresh Japanese flavours, this dish is ideally suited to outdoor, summer entertaining..

FOR THE SALMON:

4 x 150 g (1¾ oz) salmon fillets, pin bones removed

1 tablespoon kecap manis (sweet soy sauce)

1 tablespoon soy sauce

SESAME AND MIRIN DRESSING:

2 tablespoons soy sauce

2 tablespoons mirin

1 teaspoon sesame oil

2 tablespoons rice vinegar

1 tablespoon lime juice

1 teaspoon wasabi paste

1 teaspoon white sugar

freshly ground black pepper

salt to taste

½ cup vegetable oil

AVOCADO SALAD:

2 cup watercress sprigs (or rocket)

½ cup coriander (cilantro)

½ cup chervil

2 avocado, peeled and diced

1 Lebanese cucumber, finely diced

4 spring onions (scallions) trimmed and thinly sliced

2 tablespoons pickled ginger, shredded

Serves 4

SALMON METHOD:

Place salmon in a bowl and coat with the soy sauce. Set aside in the refrigerator while preparing the salad and dressing. Heat barbecue to a medium temperature and brush with vegetable oil. Place salmon on the barbecue and cook for 2–3 minutes on each side. If you prefer the fish not so rare leave on a little longer.

DRESSING METHOD:

Combine all ingredients in a bowl or blender and emulsify.

TO SERVE:

Mix all the salad ingredients in a bowl and pour over half of the dressing. Divide the salad between 4 plates and top with the salmon. Drizzle the remaining dressing over the salmon and serve.

Barbecued Chicken with Sweet Chilli Dipping Sauce

Barbecued (grilled) chicken is one of my favourite street food treats—slowly cooked over charcoal with crispy, smoky skin and moist, flavoursome flesh and often served with sweet chilli sauce. Coming back from north-east Thailand with Acland, our fearless and fluent tour leader, we stopped at a large produce market and a motorcycle vendor appeared. Set up on the back of his bike was a charcoal brazier for cooking chicken and all the ingredients and utensils for producing green papaya salad. Within 10 minutes we were sitting by the side of a 6-lane freeway enjoying a classic Issan dish of barbecued (grilled) chicken, green papaya salad and sticky rice. You don't get that by the side of the motorway in Australia!

INGREDIENTS:

1 size 16 chicken—1.6kg (2½ lb) or
    4 chicken maryland
½ teaspoon white peppercorns
6 cloves garlic, peeled
4 coriander (cilantro) roots, washed and
    scraped
2 stalks lemongrass, bottom half only,
    trimmed and finely chopped
1–2 small chillies, chopped
2 teaspoons peeled fresh turmeric or
    pinch of powdered turmeric
4 tablespoons fish sauce
2 tablespoons soy sauce
1 tablespoon palm sugar

SWEET CHILLI DIPPING SAUCE:

½ cup (125 g/4 oz) white sugar
¼ cup (60 ml/2 fl oz) rice or coconut
    vinegar
¼ cup (60 ml/2 fl oz) water
1 teaspoon salt
2 cloves garlic, peeled and crushed
¼ cup chopped coriander (cilantro) leaf
    and stem
2–6 small red chillies, finely chopped

Serves 4 or 8 as part of a selection of dishes

METHOD:

Cut the chicken into pieces or, if using maryland, cut at the joint and place in a large bowl.

Grind the peppercorns in a mortar and pestle, then add the garlic, coriander root, lemongrass, chillies and turmeric and pound to a paste. Mix with the fish sauce, soy sauce and palm sugar and add marinade to chicken pieces, rubbing to coat well. Marinate overnight or for a minimum of 2 hours. Cook slowly on a preheated moderate barbecue (grill), turning often. The chicken can also be roasted in a moderate (180°C/350°F/Gas Mark 4) oven. Transfer to a plate and serve with Sweet Chilli Dipping Sauce.

TO MAKE DIPPING SAUCE:

Combine sugar, vinegar, water and salt in a saucepan and bring to the boil, cooking over a high heat until the sauce has reduced by half. Stir in the garlic, coriander and chillies and remove from heat.

Grilled Tiger Prawns with Roasted Tomato Lemongrass Sambal

Sambals are found in many Asian cuisines and encompass relishes, chutneys and pickles. They can be simple, complex, fresh or cooked, and are traditionally part of every meal.

INGREDIENTS:

12 large tiger prawns (shrimp) peeled, deveined and heads left on

4 cloves peeled garlic

4 small hot chillies chopped

¼ cup shaoxing wine

2 tablespoons oyster sauce

¼ cup vegetable oil

TOMATO & LEMONGRASS SAMBAL:

¼ cup vegetable oil

2 punnets cherry tomatoes

2 golden shallots peeled and finely sliced

2.5 cm (1 inch) piece of ginger peeled and finely shredded

2 cloves garlic peeled and crushed

1 large red chilli finely chopped

2 tablespoons fish sauce

1 tablespoons palm sugar

2 stalks of lemongrass trimmed and thinly sliced

4 kaffir lime leaves finely shredded

squeeze of lime juice

PREPARING THE PRAWNS:

Make a paste in a mortar with the garlic and chillies. Mix in the Shaoxing wine, oyster sauce and vegetable oil. Place prawns in a large bowl and mix through the chilli marinade. Refrigerate while making the sambal.

MAKING THE SAMBAL:

Heat the oil to medium hot in a saucepan and add the cherry tomatoes, shallots, ginger, garlic and chillies. Fry gently until the tomatoes are starting to melt.

Add the fish sauce and palm sugar, lemongrass and kaffir lime leaves and cook until palm sugar dissolves. Remove from heat and stir in lime juice.

TO COOK:

Heat barbecue to medium and grill prawns until cooked. This will take 5–7 minutes depending on the size of the prawn.

TO SERVE:

Transfer to serving platter and spoon over the sambal.

Spiced Chilli Caramel Pork Fillet with Green Apple Mint Salad

If this recipe was on Facebook it would have received millions of 'likes'!

CHILLI CARAMEL PORK:

2 pork fillets trimmed of sinew

100 ml (2¾ fl oz) tamarind water

30 ml (1fl oz) whisky

200 g (7 oz) palm sugar chopped

50 ml (1¾ fl oz) fish sauce

25 ml (1fl oz) dark soy sauce

2 cloves garlic peeled and crushed

1 large red chilli chopped

zest and juice of 1 lime

APPLE AND MINT SALAD:

2 teaspoons palm sugar chopped

2 tablespoons lime juice

1 green apple, skin on and finely
  shredded

½ cup bean sprouts topped and tailed

3 spring onions (scallions) trimmed and
  finely sliced

1 large red chilli deseeded and finely
  sliced

1 tablespoon ginger peeled and finely
  shredded

1 cup washed mint leaves

Serves 4

PREPARING THE PORK:

Place tamarind water, whisky, palm sugar, fish sauce, soy sauce, garlic, chilli and lime zest in a saucepan and bring to the boil. Reduce to a simmer and cook until slightly syrupy – about five minutes. Remove from heat, stir in lime juice and set aside to cool.

When cold, marinate the pork in half of the sauce while preparing the salad. Set the remainder aside to pour over the cooked pork.

SALAD METHOD:

In a large bowl combine palm sugar and lime juice and stir to dissolve the sugar. Add the remaining ingredients and toss gently to mix.

TO COOK AND SERVE:

Heat the barbecue to medium. Grill the pork fillet, brushing with the sauce. Take care not to burn and turn often. This will take about 20–25 minutes to cook. Rest for 10 minutes. Then slice into 1 cm thick medallions and transfer to serving platter. Reheat the remaining sauce and pour over pork. Serve with green apple salad on the side.

Mains

Curried Rice with Chicken & Fresh Cucumber Pickle

The first time I enjoyed this was in Hat Yai, a lively but slightly seedy town just over the Thai border from Malaysia. Hat Yai is a mecca for Muslim food, including roti and spice-dominated curries. This is a pilaf-style dish, with the chicken and spices braised in the rice. It's sometimes served with a bowl of broth or a simple pickle.

INGREDIENTS:

4 cloves garlic, peeled

2 tablespoons ginger, peeled and chopped

1 tablespoon fresh turmeric, peeled and chopped (if unavailable, use a teaspoon of powdered turmeric)

1 teaspoon salt

1 tablespoon curry powder

4 chicken thighs, cut in half

1 cup (250 ml/8 fl oz) vegetable oil

4 golden shallots, peeled and thinly sliced

3 cups jasmine rice, rinsed and drained

4 cups (1 l/34 fl oz) chicken stock

½ cinnamon stick

CUCUMBER PICKLE:

½ cup (125 ml/4 fl oz) coconut or rice vinegar

¼ cup (60 g/2 oz) white sugar

1 teaspoon salt

1 small Lebanese cucumber

2 small golden shallots, peeled and sliced

2–4 small red chillies, thinly sliced

Serves 4 or 8 as part of a selection of dishes

METHOD:

Make a paste with the garlic, ginger, turmeric and salt, then mix with the curry powder. Place chicken in a bowl and coat with the spice paste. Set aside for an hour or two in the refrigerator.

Heat a cup of oil in a wok to medium and fry the shallots until golden and crispy.

Drain on paper towel. Transfer 4 tablespoons of the oil into a heavy-based saucepan and brown the chicken. Add the rice, stock and cinnamon. Bring to the boil, stirring once or twice, then turn down to a very low heat, cover and cook for 20 minutes. Transfer to a serving plate and garnish with the reserved crispy shallots. Serve with Cucumber Pickle.

TO MAKE THE PICKLE:

Combine the vinegar, sugar and salt in a saucepan. Take off heat as soon as sugar has dissolved. Allow to cool completely.

Cut the cucumber lengthways and then finely dice. Combine in a bowl with the shallots, chillies and cooled vinegar syrup.

Braised Pork With Sweet Soy, Cinnamon, Star Anise & Ginger

Found on street food stalls throughout Thailand, this popular dish, which cooks pork shoulders in large vats, lures hungry customers with its wafts of cinnamon and star anise.

INGREDIENTS:

2 tablespoons vegetable oil

5 red shallots, peeled and sliced

5 cloves garlic, peeled and chopped

650 g (1 lb 5 oz) pork neck, cut into
    2.5 cm (1 inch) cubes

1 knob ginger, peeled and julienned

3 tablespoons kecap manis (sweet
    soy sauce)

2 tablespoons soy sauce

1 teaspoon ground white pepper

2 cups chicken stock

a few small red chillies, left whole

1 cinnamon stick

2 star anise

Serves 4

METHOD:

Heat oil in a wok. Add the shallots and garlic and sauté for 2 minutes over low heat.

Turn heat to high and add pork and cook until pork is sealed.

Add remaining ingredients and simmer over medium heat for about 45 minutes. When cooked there should be very little sauce left and the meat should have a rich shine glaze.

If it dries out too much during cooking add a little more chicken stock or water. When cooked transfer to serving plates, serve with jasmine rice and steamed vegetables.

Steamed Salmon with Spicy Black Bean & Ginger Paste

Sometimes the simplest recipes are the most popular. This modern Asian dish has always been a 'hit' in Spirit House cooking classes. Any good quality fish fillets can be substituted for the salmon.

INGREDIENTS:

6 x 150 g (5 oz) portions salmon

1 large red chilli, de-seeded (pitted) and shredded thinly for garnish

coriander (cilantro) sprigs for garnish

Spicy Black Bean and Ginger Paste

2 tablespoons dried, salted black beans

90 ml (3 fl oz) vegetable oil

2 tablespoons ginger, peeled and grated

4 cloves garlic, crushed

1 large red chilli, finely chopped

2 tablespoons sweet soy sauce

2 tablespoons palm sugar

1 teaspoon ground black pepper

Serves 6

METHOD:

Place the salmon on a plate that fits into a steamer basket. Divide the black bean sauce between the salmon portions and steam, covered, for 6–7 minutes. Transfer to serving plates and garnish with the red chilli and coriander leaves.

TO MAKE PASTE:

Soak the black beans in ¾ cup warm water for 10 minutes, then squeeze out water and chop the beans finely. Reserve the soaking water. Heat the vegetable oil and fry the ginger, garlic and chilli until soft and fragrant but not brown. Add the black beans, soy sauce, palm sugar and pepper and cook on a low heat until the sugar has dissolved. Moisten with some of the reserved black bean soaking water. The mixture should be liquid but thick.

Five Spice Pork with Chinese Spiced Plum Sauce

Grown men have been known to cry when plums go out of season and Spirit House chefs remove this dish from the menu.

MASTER STOCK:

3 L (5¼ pints) water

20 ml (¾ fl oz) dark soy

50 ml (1¾ fl oz) thin soy sauce

125 ml (4½ fl oz) Shaoxing wine

100 g (3½ oz) yellow rock sugar

¼ cup peeled and sliced ginger

¼ cup garlic, peeled

2 star anise

2 pieces cassia bark

2 pieces tangerine peel

FIVE SPICE PORK:

1½ kg (3 lb) pork belly, skin-on and bone removed

2 tablespoons Chinese five spice

2 tablespoons sea salt

1 tablespoon ground white pepper

butcher's twine

quantity of master stock (above)

12 plum halves

2 bunches of bok choy or Asian green vegetables

PLUM SAUCE:

500 g (1 lb) light palm sugar

100 ml (3½ fl oz) water

100 ml (3½ fl oz) fish sauce

100 ml (3½ fl oz) tamarind water
   (100 g tamarind pulp dissolved in
   100 ml warm water, then strained)

100 g (¼ oz) Hoisin sauce

10 cut whole plums

Serves 6

Recipe continues on page 124

TO MAKE MASTER STOCK:

Bring all to boil, simmer on low heat for 1 hour. Strain and discard ingredients.

The stock will become intense in flavour over time, so just dilute with a little water.

TO MAKE FIVE SPICE PORK:

Mix the five spice with salt and white pepper.

Rub the inside (non skin side) of the pork with the five spice mix.

Roll the pork lengthways and tie tightly with butcher twine approx every 5 cm (2 inches) along the pork.

Bring master stock to boil. Place the pork in an ovenproof dish or pot. Pour simmering master stock over the pork, making sure pork is completely covered. Cover the dish with baking paper and then foil to seal. Place in 160°C (325°F/Gas Mark 3) oven for 2½ hours.

Remove pork from master stock and place on a tray to cool in fridge overnight.

Cut pork into portions approx 250 g (8 oz) each.

TO MAKE FIVE PLUM SAUCE:

Melt sugar in water in a heavy based pot until sugar starts to caramelise.

Add fish sauce, tamarind water, Hoisin sauce and plums and cook until plums are very soft and the sauce has a honey consistency. Strain.

TO SERVE:

Stir-fry the bok choy and portion on to individual serving plates.

Fry pork portions in deep fryer on 180°C (350°F/Gas Mark 4) until gold and warm all the way through. Slice pork and arrange the slices on top of the stir-fried green vegetables. Pour plum sauce over and garnish with plum cheeks that have warmed in the sauce.

Whole Fish Grilled in Banana Leaf with Pickled Plum, Ginger & Spring Onions

This is another dish that has its roots in China but has been adapted by the Thais. The pickled green plums are about the size of a cumquat and, despite the name, are actually a type of apricot. The best brands come from China and they impart a distinctive sour and salty note to the dish.
If banana leaves are unavailable, simply replace with baking paper.

INGREDIENTS:

1 whole fish about 600–700 g (21–25 oz), cleaned

2 coriander (cilantro) roots, washed and scraped

2 green spring onions (scallions), white part sliced thinly, green part sliced thinly for garnish

4 pickled plums, pitted and roughly chopped

2 tablespoons pickled plum juice

1 tablespoon fish sauce

1 tablespoon light soy sauce

½ teaspoon white sugar

¼ cup ginger, peeled and finely shredded

handful of coriander (cilantro) leaves for garnish

1 large red chilli, de-seeded (pitted) and julienned for garnish

Serves 4–6 as part of a selection of dishes

METHOD:

Make three diagonal slashes on the fish and put the coriander roots into its cavity. In a bowl, mix together the plums, pickled plum juice, fish sauce, soy sauce and sugar.

Place the fish on a banana leaf and spoon the combined sauce over the fish. Sprinkle the fish with the white part of the spring onion and the shredded ginger. Fold the banana leaf over and then wrap the package in aluminium foil.

Cook on a preheated barbecue (grill), turning a few times, for about 20 minutes.

Carefully open the foil package, taking care not to lose any of the cooking juices. Transfer the fish to a serving platter and pour over the reserved juices. Garnish with the reserved green spring onion, coriander leaves and red chillies.

Poached Red Snapper with Hot & Sour Herb Salad

A fragrant, delicate broth to honour an expensive piece of wild caught seafood.
A classic example of keep it simple!

POACHING LIQUID:

150 ml (7 fl oz) fish sauce
150 ml (7 fl oz) lime juice
100 g (3 ½ oz) palm sugar
100 ml (3 ½ fl oz) water

HOT AND SOUR HERB SALAD:

4 red chillies
4 green chillies
2 birds eye chillies
6 garlic cloves
4 coriander (cilantro) roots, cleaned
1 cup coriander (cilantro) leaves
½ cup mint leaves

Serves 6

TO POACH LIQUID:

Place fish sauce, lime juice, palm sugar and water in a small saucepan and heat until sugar is dissolved.

Pour all, except for 2 tablespoons, of liquid mixture over the fish fillets and place in baking dish, cover with foil and steam in a moderate oven for approximately 10–12 minutes.

TO MAKE SALAD:

Pound chillies, garlic and coriander root in mortar and pestle with remaining 2 tablespoons of poaching liquid. Mix with coriander and mint leaves and garnish fish with this salad.

Whole Crispy Fish with Roasted Chilli Paste & Lemongrass

Whole crispy fish has been on the Spirit House restaurant menu since Day One. It has an amazing 'wow factor' when placed on the table and is almost the Spirit House signature dish. This dish is a good example of how Westerners sometimes misunderstand certain characteristics of Asian food—in this case it's the textural component. Crispy, bouncy, chewy, rubbery and sticky are not usually desirable characteristics in Western cooking, but they certainly play an important role in Asian food. I will always remember my first complaint about the crispy fish: 'This fish is all dry and overcooked.' But that's the whole point.

The dish is not meant to be eaten on its own but as part of a selection of dishes to be shared and enjoyed for its chewy, crispy texture. The following recipe is based on a whole crispy fish we had riverside in the old Thai capital of Ayutthaya.

INGREDIENTS:

1 whole firm fleshed white fish about 750 g (1.5 lb), scaled and gutted, for example red emperor or gold band snapper

4 cups (1 L/34 fl oz) vegetable oil

SAUCE:

2 stalks lemongrass, finely chopped, bottom half only and outer leaves removed

8 kaffir lime leaves

2 teaspoons light palm sugar

2 tablespoons fish sauce

2 tablespoons tamarind water

4 tablespoons roasted chilli paste

½ cup (125 ml/4 fl oz) chicken stock or water

½ cup Thai basil leaves

1 large red chilli, de-seeded (pitted) and thinly sliced

Serves 6–8 as part of a selection of dishes

METHOD:

Dry the fish well inside and out with a paper towel. Crosshatch with deep diagonal cuts almost to the bone.

Heat the oil in a wok to medium high and carefully lower the fish into the oil. Take care initially, as it can splatter. Baste the fish with oil while cooking and after about 7–10 minutes carefully turn over and cook another 5 minutes. Remove from the wok and drain on a paper towel.

Transfer to a serving plate and pour the prepared sauce over it.

TO MAKE THE SAUCE:

Combine the lemongrass, kaffir lime leaves, palm sugar, fish sauce, tamarind water, roasted chilli paste and stock or water in a small saucepan and bring to the boil, stirring until the sugar has dissolved. Add the basil leaves and chilli. Remove from heat as soon as the basil has wilted.

Red Braised Duck
with Lychee & Ginger Salad

Duck is the most popular main course on the Spirit House menu. Many home cooks are intimidated by it, but if you use the leg and thigh cuts, it's no harder than cooking a casserole. These cuts are sold as duck maryland and will be available from good butchers or supermarkets. The technique of red braising is classically Chinese. The red refers to the glossy mahogany colour that the meat takes on from the soy sauces.
Start this dish in the morning or the day before, as the stock needs to be chilled so the duck fat can be removed.

INGREDIENTS:

4 duck maryland

all of the master stock from recipe below

2 green spring onions (scallions), including some of the green part, trimmed and thinly sliced

12 lychees, peeled, de-seeded (pitted) and halved

½ cup mint leaves

½ cup coriander (cilantro) leaves

½ red chilli, de-seeded (pitted) and finely shredded

2 tablespoons ginger, peeled and finely shredded 4 kaffir lime leaves, finely shredded juice of half a lime

MASTER STOCK:

2 L (3½ pints) of water

250 ml (8 fl oz) Shaoxing wine

125 ml (4 fl oz) light soy sauce

75 ml (2½ fl oz/⅓ cup) dark soy sauce

100 g (3½ oz) yellow rock sugar

2 pieces tangerine peel

2 pieces cassia bark

4 pieces star anise

1 knob ginger, roughly chopped

4 cloves garlic, peeled

METHOD:

To make master stock: Bring all the ingredients to boil in a large stock pot, simmer for half an hour. Strain. Makes about 2½ litres (4 pints). Any leftover master stock can be either refrigerated for up to a week or frozen for several months. Use as a base for soups, add a few spoonfuls to a stir-fry or use for braising meats.

TO PREPARE DUCK:

Preheat oven to 160°C (325°F/Gas Mark 3).

Trim excess fat from the duck and cut at the joint. Place in a baking dish, skin side down. Bring master stock to the boil in a saucepan and pour over the duck pieces so they are almost submerged. Cover with a lid or aluminium foil and place in oven. Cook for 1½ hours and then remove the lid or foil and turn ducks over to skin side up.

Cook for another hour until the meat is almost falling from the bone. Remove the duck from the stock and refrigerate until needed. Completely chill the master stock in the refrigerator and then remove the fat that will have set on top.

Place stock in a saucepan, bring to the boil and reduce by half. The duck pieces can be either reheated in the reduced stock or, for crispy skin duck, placed in a shallow pan, skin side up with a little stock, then reheated uncovered in a 180°C (350°F/Gas Mark 4) oven.

While the duck is reheating and the sauce reducing, make the salad by combining the remaining ingredients in a bowl and tossing with a squeeze of lime juice.

Transfer duck pieces to serving bowl and pour over about ½ cup (125 ml/4 fl oz) of reduced stock, then pile the lychee and ginger salad on top of the duck pieces.

Serves 4 or 8 as part of a selection of dishes

Beef Shin Braised with Red Dates & Shiitake Mushrooms

This beef stew has the intense flavour of dried shiitake mushrooms plus the richness of red dates—an ideal dish for a cold winter's night. Red dates are also known as jujubes and have been cultivated in China for thousands of years. They can be dried, candied or eaten fresh and are also important in Chinese medicine where they are considered to be calming and good for circulation. Red dates can be found in Asian supermarkets. If unavailable, omit rather than substituting with the common date.

INGREDIENTS:

2 tablespoons vegetable oil

600 g (21 oz) diced beef shin or other stewing beef

3 cloves garlic, peeled and minced (ground)

3 tablespoons ginger, peeled and minced (ground)

1 tablespoon chilli bean sauce 1 medium tomato, diced

2 tablespoons Shaoxing wine

2 tablespoons yellow rock sugar

2 tablespoons soy sauce

1 tablespoon oyster sauce

500 ml (16 fl oz/2 cups) water

8 Chinese red dates

4 dried shiitake mushrooms, stems removed and soaked in boiling water until soft, then thinly sliced

Serves 4–6, or 8–10 as part of a selection of dishes

METHOD:

In a heavy-based pot, heat the oil and brown the meat. Add the remaining ingredients and bring to the boil. Reduce to a low simmer and cook, uncovered, until the meat is tender. This will take about 2 hours if using beef shin. The sauce should be reduced and thick when finished.

Transfer meat to serving bowls and serve with steamed jasmine rice.

Desserts

Mangoes with Sticky Rice & Coconut Cream

The one Thai dessert everyone knows and loves! Sesame seeds add a crunchy texture to the juicy soft mangoes.

INGREDIENTS:

2 cups sticky rice

water

750 ml (24 fl oz) coconut cream

few drops of vanilla essence or a vanilla
  bean

1¼ cup of castor sugar

½ teaspoon salt

3 mangoes to serve 6 people

1 tablespoon sesame seeds for garnish

Serves 6 or 4, if this is your favourite

METHOD:

Cover sticky rice with cold water and soak overnight. Drain and steam for approximately 30–40 minutes in steamer basket lined with clean cloth over boiling water.

Set aside half cup of coconut cream. Combine remaining coconut cream with sugar, salt and vanilla, stir over gentle heat in a saucepan (not aluminium) until sugar is dissolved.

Transfer cooked rice to large bowl. Pour over coconut cream mixture. Set aside until rice has absorbed all the coconut cream. Divide rice and mangoes between serving plates. Spoon remaining coconut cream over rice and garnish with toasted sesame seeds.

Palm Sugar & Lemongrass Panna cotta

This panna cotta is extremely easy to make and simple to jazz up for a dinner party, by serving with some fresh fruits, jellies or sorbet. You can put your own twist on this recipe by changing the lemongrass with any Asian aromatic or spice.

INGREDIENTS:

2 large stalks of lemongrass
440 ml (14 fl oz) whipping cream
150 ml (5 fl oz) full-cream milk
75 g (2½ oz) palm sugar
45 g (1½ oz) caster sugar
2 leaves gelatine

TO SERVE:

1 stalk lemongrass
Sprigs of micro mint leaves

Serves 8

METHOD:

Bruise the lemongrass by hitting repeatedly with the back of a knife, pestle or meat mallet. Place the lemongrass, cream and milk into a saucepan and warm over a low heat. Once warm, add both palm sugar and caster (superfine) sugar and stir until the sugar is dissolved. Bring mixture to a light simmer for 20 minutes. remove mixture from heat, cover and let the flavours infuse for half an hour.

After 20 minutes, soak the gelatine in some cold water for 5 minutes to allow it to soften. Place the panna cotta mixture back onto the heat and return to a simmer. Squeeze out any excess water from the gelatine and add the gelatine to the mixture. Stir until dissolved and strain the mixture through a fine sieve. Pour the panna cotta mixture into eight dariole moulds or ramekins and refrigerate for four hours or until set.

TO SERVE:

Run a small knife, dipped into very hot water, around the inside of each mould and turn the panna cotta out into the centre of each serving plate. Garnish simply with some very finely julienned rings of lemongrass and sprigs of micro mint leaves.

Chilli Chocolate Brownie

A spicy blend of chilli and chocolate makes these brownies a decadent companion to serve with an after-dinner coffee.

INGREDIENTS:

225 g (8 oz) dark chocolate, broken into chunks

140 g (5 oz) unsalted butter

200 g (7 oz) caster (superfine) sugar

1 teaspoon (5 g) vanilla extract

½ teaspoon (2.5 g) ground star anise

¼ teaspoon medium heat chilli powder

45 g (1½ oz) pine nuts

1 punnet fresh raspberries

2 eggs

1 egg yolk

85 g (3 oz) plain flour, sifted dutch cocoa powder, for dusting

METHOD:

Preheat oven to 180°C (350°F/Gas Mark 4). Line a 20 cm (7¾ in) square tray with baking paper.

In a heatproof bowl, place 200 g (7 oz) of the chocolate and all the butter and melt over a pan of simmering water. Stir once, making sure the butter and chocolate have completely melted. Stir in sugar, vanilla, star anise, chilli powder, pine nuts, raspberries and the extra chocolate chunks. Mix well, then add the eggs and sifted flour.

Bake for 35 minutes then cool, cut into desired size pieces.

TO SERVE:

Dust with dutch cocoa powder. Serve with freshly brewed coffee or tea.

Ginger, Coconut & Tapioca Pudding, Roasted Pineapple & Candied Ginger Chips

Here tapioca pearls make a wonderfully creamy gluten-free dessert. The chewy little pearls are a lovely contrast to the smooth coconut and the natural sweetness of the roasted pineapple

ROASTED PINEAPPLE:

½ pineapple
45 g (1½ oz) brown sugar
60 ml (2 fl oz) orange juice
20 g (⅔ oz) honey

FOR THE PUDDING:

140 g (5 oz) small tapioca pearls
500 ml (16 fl oz) milk
500 ml (16 fl oz) coconut cream
160 g (5½) castor sugar
1 vanilla bean, split lengthways
¼ cup candied ginger, diced

TO MAKE ROASTED PINEAPPLE:

Preheat the oven to 220°C (420°F/Gas Mark 7). Line a tray with baking paper. Peel and core the pineapple and cut into 2 cm (¾ in) pieces. In a bowl, whisk together the sugar, orange juice and honey.

Add pineapple pieces and toss to coat. Spread the pineapple over the tray and roast in the oven for 30 minutes, or until tender and caramelised. Remove from the oven, drizzle over any remaining sugar mixture and allow to cool. Store in an airtight container in the refrigerator for 3 days.

TO MAKE THE PUDDING:

Soak the tapioca in cold water for 20 minutes, strain and discard the water.

In a large saucepan, stir the milk, coconut cream, sugar, vanilla bean and tapioca over a low heat until the tapioca is translucent. Stir in diced candied ginger.

TO SERVE:

Portion the tapioca pudding into six 125 ml (4 fl oz) serving bowls. Top with some warm Roasted Pineapple and sprinkle over with Candied Ginger Chips (see page 149).

Candied Ginger Chips

Small sweet ginger chips that pack a deceivingly big kick of heat. Scatter sparingly across Ginger and Tapioca puddings.

INGREDIENTS:

20 g (⅔ oz) ginger, peeled

100 g (3½ oz) caster (superfine) sugar

100 ml (2¾ fl oz) water

Makes enough candy to garnish 6 desserts

METHOD:

Preheat the oven to its lowest setting and line an oven tray with baking paper. Thinly slice the ginger diagonally across its fibres.

Place the sugar and water into a saucepan over a medium heat and bring to a simmer. Once the sugar has dissolved, place ginger slices into the syrup and stir until well coated.

Remove from heat and strain ginger out of the syrup. (Reserve the syrup and use it to drizzle over any dessert for a hint of sweet ginger, it will keep in the refrigerator for up to one month.)

Using two forks, spread the individual ginger slices out flat, spaced apart across the oven tray. Place the tray in the oven and allow to dry overnight.

Store candied ginger chips in an airtight container, away from moisture for up to 1 month.

Chocolate Brûlée with Chilli Raspberry Jam, Chilli Candy & Chocolate Brandy snap

A dessert menu favourite—lush silken chocolate, burnt sugar, splash of raspberry and chilli.

CHOCOLATE BRÛLÉE:

8 egg yolks

75 g (2½ oz) caster (superfine) sugar

500 ml (16 fl oz) cream

1 vanilla bean, cut in half lengthways
   and scraped

150 g (5oz) dark chocolate, chopped

extra sugar for caramelising

CHILLI RASPBERRY JAM:

5 long red chillies (deseeded)

250 g (8½ oz) frozen raspberries

250 g (8½ oz) palm sugar

TO SERVE:

strips of chilli candy
   (see page 157)

6 chocolate Brandy Snaps
   (see page 155)

Serves 6

CHOCOLATE BRÛLÉE:

Whisk eggs and sugar in a heatproof bowl until thick and creamy.

Pour cream into a saucepan, add vanilla bean and bring to just on boiling point. Pour onto egg mix and whisk well, pour back into saucepan and stir over low heat until the mix looks very thick and a bit like scrambled eggs. Take off the heat and whisk in chocolate. remove vanilla bean.

Blend mix with a stick blender until smooth and glossy, then pass through a fine strainer.

CHILLI RASPBERRY JAM:

Blend chillies in a food processor, then add to raspberries and palm sugar in a saucepan. Bring to a simmer and cook on low heat for half an hour or until a thick jam. Then let cool.

TO SERVE:

Place 1 teaspoon of raspberry chilli jam on the bottom of each ramekin. Fill with the chocolate mix. Sprinkle 1 tablespoon of sugar on top of each brûlée. Fire up a blowtorch and caramelise the sugar.

Garnish with some strips of chilli candy on top of the cooled sugar.

Serve with a chocolate Brandy Snap on the side of the plate.

Spiced Coconut Cake with Tropical Fruits & Palm Sugar Sauce

A deliciously simple cake! Everything is mixed in one bowl, resulting in a very Asian Style texture with a crisp coconut topping.

CAKE:

180 g (6 oz) butter, melted

1½ cups caster sugar

¾ cup plain flour

1½ cups shredded coconut

6 eggs

½ teaspoon ground nutmeg

½ teaspoon cinnamon

SYRUP:

125 g (4 oz) dark palm sugar

3 tablespoons water

½ cup coconut cream

FRUIT:

1 red pawpaw, peeled, cut into 2.5 cm
   (1 in) chunks

12 lychees, peeled and pitted

pulp of 4 passionfruit

Serves 12

METHOD:

To make the cake, combine all the cake ingredients in a large bowl and mix well.

Pour mixture into a greased, lined 24 cm (10 in) springform pan. Bake at 165°C (325°F/ Gas Mark 3) for 40–45 minutes or until cooked when tested with a skewer.

Cool in pan for 10 minutes before turning out onto a rack to cool.

TO MAKE THE SYRUP:

Combine the palm sugar, water and coconut cream in a pan.

Bring to the boil and simmer until syrupy, about 5–10 minutes.

To serve, place slices of the coconut cake on individual plates with red pawpaw and lychees. Drizzle the syrup and passionfruit pulp over the fruit and cake. Dust cake lightly with icing sugar.

Chocolate Brandy Snap

Serve with Chocolate Desserts or Ice Cream, or as a garnish for the Chocolate Brûlée with Raspberry Chilli Jam

INGREDIENTS:

225 g (8 oz) caster (superfine) sugar
125 g (4 oz) unsalted butter
4 tablespoons (60 g) glucose syrup
100 g (3½ oz) plain (all-purpose) flour
25 g (¾ oz) cocoa powder
Preheat oven to 160°C (325°F/Gas Mark 3)

Makes approximately 20 snaps

METHOD:

Melt sugar, butter and glucose in a saucepan over low heat, do not colour. Take off the heat and add sifted flour and cocoa powder.

Roll into logs about ¾ in (2 cm) in diameter, refrigerate until firm. Cut thin slices and place onto baking tray, six at a time. Cook for about 8 minutes until mixture bubbles. Remove from oven and curl around the end of a wooden spoon.

Store in refrigerator in airtight container lined with baking paper for up to 1 week.